AMERICANS

IN SPACE

BY THE EDITORS OF
AMERICAN HERITAGE
The Magazine of History

AUTHOR
JOHN DILLE

CONSULTANT
PHILIP S. HOPKINS
Former Director, National Air Museum, Smithsonian Institution

PUBLISHED BY
AMERICAN HERITAGE PUBLISHING CO., INC.

BOOK TRADE AND INSTITUTIONAL DISTRIBUTION BY
HARPER & ROW

In 1961, pressure was on to design, produce, and deliver Mercury space capsules on schedule. Here, technicians in a sterile room check capsules against dust and small particles that might interfere with their electrical systems.

FOREWORD

Americans have always been a space-minded people: to explore the vast reaches of our land and to probe the sky and waters around it have been a historic American concern. Benjamin Franklin, when watching the first balloon ascension in Paris, was asked of what possible good such an air-borne contraption might be. The great inventor, looking upward, replied, "Of what good is a newborn baby?"

This book tells the story of the first major step taken by Americans into space, a period of our history that lasted roughly from 1914 to 1963. It was a period of experimentation, frustration, and ultimate triumph. It was opened by a secretive physics professor in Worcester, Massachusetts, whose rockets were regarded in some quarters as little more than public menaces; it was given impetus by the technology of World War II; and it was concluded by the sensational feats of Project Mercury.

Because the nation's current space programs have gone on to produce new vehicles and new challenges, the mechanisms and the words of that early era seem antique. The adjective "A-OK" has long since been added to the lexicon of cast-off phrases; the Mercury capsules being carefully readied by technicians in the "white room" in the photograph on the opposite page seem ready only for a museum.

But the result of that historic effort is that today the second step into space is considered desirable and humanly possible. And if anyone asks why we want to try for the moon or venture into the space beyond, we may answer (with some greater experience, but no greater wisdom, than Franklin): because we know that we can.

The Editors

A number of AMERICAN HERITAGE
JUNIOR LIBRARY *books are published each year.*
Titles currently available are:

AMERICANS IN SPACE
ABRAHAM LINCOLN IN PEACE AND WAR
AIR WAR AGAINST HITLER'S GERMANY
IRONCLADS OF THE CIVIL WAR
THE ERIE CANAL
THE MANY WORLDS OF BENJAMIN FRANKLIN
COMMODORE PERRY IN JAPAN
THE BATTLE OF GETTYSBURG
ANDREW JACKSON, SOLDIER AND STATESMAN
ADVENTURES IN THE WILDERNESS
LEXINGTON, CONCORD AND BUNKER HILL
CLIPPER SHIPS AND CAPTAINS
D-DAY, THE INVASION OF EUROPE
WESTWARD ON THE OREGON TRAIL
THE FRENCH AND INDIAN WARS
GREAT DAYS OF THE CIRCUS
STEAMBOATS ON THE MISSISSIPPI
COWBOYS AND CATTLE COUNTRY
TEXAS AND THE WAR WITH MEXICO
THE PILGRIMS AND PLYMOUTH COLONY
THE CALIFORNIA GOLD RUSH
PIRATES OF THE SPANISH MAIN
TRAPPERS AND MOUNTAIN MEN
MEN OF SCIENCE AND INVENTION
NAVAL BATTLES AND HEROES
THOMAS JEFFERSON AND HIS WORLD
DISCOVERERS OF THE NEW WORLD
RAILROADS IN THE DAYS OF STEAM
INDIANS OF THE PLAINS
THE STORY OF YANKEE WHALING

American Heritage also publishes
HORIZON CARAVEL BOOKS, *a similar series*
on world history, culture, and the arts.
Titles currently available are:

THE FRENCH REVOLUTION
CORTES AND THE AZTEC CONQUEST
CAESAR
THE UNIVERSE OF GALILEO AND NEWTON
THE VIKINGS
MARCO POLO'S ADVENTURES IN CHINA
SHAKESPEARE'S ENGLAND
CAPTAIN COOK AND THE SOUTH PACIFIC
THE SEARCH FOR EARLY MAN
JOAN OF ARC
EXPLORATION OF AFRICA
NELSON AND THE AGE OF FIGHTING SAIL
ALEXANDER THE GREAT
RUSSIA UNDER THE CZARS
HEROES OF POLAR EXPLORATION
KNIGHTS OF THE CRUSADES

RIGHT: *The last Mercury astronaut was Gordon Cooper, who had just "suited up" for flight on May 15, 1963, when Robert McCall sketched him.*

NASA

COVER: *The first American to blast into space was Alan Shepard. He walks from his transport van toward the hissing rocket that will carry him up.*

Paris Match FROM PICTORIAL PARADE

ENDSHEETS: *Roaring above the huge gantries and the scrubby land of Cape Kennedy, an Atlas rocket lifts skyward, taking John Glenn into orbit.*

Life MAGAZINE (C) 1962 TIME INC.

TITLE PAGE: *Ballooning was already an American pastime when this photograph of the Gordon Bennett International Balloon Race was taken in 1907.*

U.S. AIR FORCE

CONTENTS

1

THE LURE OF SPACE

In 1834 enthusiastic Americans saluted a balloonist over Baltimore.

Shortly before John Glenn became the first American to orbit the earth and spend several hours in space, he explained to a friend why he was risking his life to go on this great adventure. "I feel we astronauts have been given a great opportunity to add to man's knowledge," he said. "And I guess there is something of the pioneer in all of us. We are starting to explore the unknown frontier that surrounds us in space. We are just about where Columbus was when he set sail across an uncharted ocean, and where Charles Lindbergh was when he took off on the first solo flight across the Atlantic. We are plunging into something so new that no one is sure just what we will find or how it will work out."

In April, 1959, when Glenn and the six other original astronauts (Scott Carpenter, Gordon Cooper, Virgil Grissom, Walter Schirra, Alan Shep-

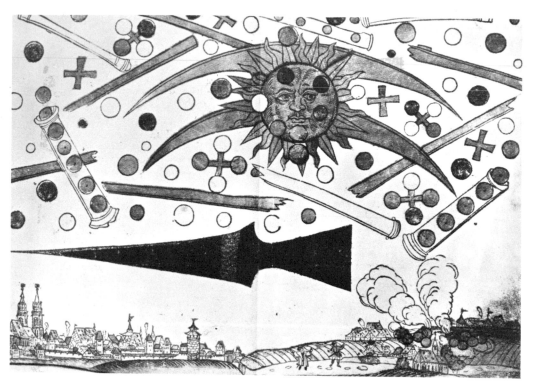

In this sixteenth-century battle scene, the sun's face is marked with blood spots—regarded as a sign of hope by the troops below.

ard, and Donald Slayton) joined Project Mercury, the first U.S. program for putting men into space was still in the planning stages. But man's urge to venture into space was not. It was an ancient instinct that must have occurred to primitive man when he saw the stars twinkling above him at night or felt the hot sun burn his flesh during the day.

In the very early days of human life on earth, men and women could not help being afraid of the heavens. For here the ferocious lightning flashed. And from the heavens the distant stars seemed to blink on and off behind the misty clouds. From here came the great storms that could either wet the crops and make them grow—or drown the fields and people's homes in terrible floods. And here moved the huge sun that could either warm the earth and nourish the crops—or burn the fields to a crisp and leave the people starving. These were all such mysteries and so far from man's reach that they were beyond his understanding.

But then, as the centuries passed and later generations had more time to study their surroundings, people began to understand something about space. The earliest astronomers, for example, learned how to plot the paths of the sun and the moon and thereby tell the division of the year into seasons and months, days and hours. Navigators became so familiar with the twinkling lights overhead that they began giving each star a name drawn from myth or religion. And when sailors realized that the stars formed a fixed pattern, they started to use the lights of the night sky as trusted beacons from which they could take their bearings.

The ancient Mediterranean and Near Eastern civilizations pioneered in this kind of knowledge. As long ago as 300 B.C., a Greek astronomer named Aristarchus of Samos came to the conclusion from observing the heavens with his naked eye—there were no telescopes then—that the sun stood still while the earth and the other planets revolved around it. This, Aristarchus said, explains the passing of night and day and the changing seasons. This fact seems obvious today. But in ancient times, when scientific knowledge was limited, not everybody agreed.

More than 300 years after Aristarchus, the Greek-Egyptian astronomer Ptolemy completely contradicted him and claimed it was the earth that stood still, with the sun, moon, and stars revolving around *it*. The bodies all moved at the same speed, he said, and in perfect circular orbits.

Ptolemy also decided—again without any telescopes to help him—that the universe was made up of a series of globes, one inside the other. (In attempting to make a diagram of the universe, space, and the solar system, Ptolemy concluded that such an overlapping structure was necessary.) Each globe was formed, he said, of a different kind of element. The innermost globe was the earth, and the others consisted successively of water, air, fire, and gas. Ptolemy was only guessing, of course, and his theory was completely wrong. But many people wanted to believe that their earth was at the center of everything, so Ptolemy's ideas were accepted. They remained almost unchallenged, in fact, for several centuries.

At about the same time, other scientists were making equally wrong guesses about the earth itself. Early medieval maps, for example, showed much of Africa as an uninhabited land that was so fiercely hot it gave off huge flames and was surrounded by great seas of boiling water. Though some

To the Hopis of Arizona, the sun was a god.

traders and explorers had ventured into it, the Atlantic Ocean was often pictured as a spooky, dark chasm where no light ever shone. It was no wonder that early seafarers avoided these areas as long as they could.

But then, about 500 years ago, people's ideas on all these subjects began to change a great deal. Explorers like Columbus and Magellan made their great voyages, searching for the fabulous riches of the Orient that Marco Polo had discovered on his journey across Asia two centuries before. Other sailors, some inspired by Portugal's Prince Henry the Navigator, ventured down the coast of Africa in search of treasure and knowledge in that direction. Slowly the people began to realize that their illustrated maps were wrong and that the earth was not such a treacherous, mysterious place after all.

With this new burst of activity came new ideas, and scientists began correcting their mistaken notions about all kinds of things. The period during which most of this took place is known as the Renaissance, and it lasted from about 1400 to 1650. During this productive time, scientists and teachers discarded many of the superstitions and errors that had been handed down to them from one generation to another and that had seriously hampered their thinking. New ideas were bubbling up everywhere—in music, painting , literature, and science.

In the scientific world the names of four great men stand out. Each of

In the fifteenth century, so little was known of the earth that a fiery-red Africa (at bottom on this Venetian map) was described as "uninhabited because of heat and dragons."

An engraving of 1661 (opposite) illustrates Copernicus' theory that the earth orbits around the sun. A more accurate clockwork model of the solar system (left) was built for Harvard University in 1787 by a Boston watchmaker. Paul Revere may have cast the figures of famous scientists, including Newton (right of center) and Franklin (left of center), which surround the instrument's stand.

these thinkers made a tremendously important contribution to our present understanding of space and the universe. And each, in his own way, helped to make space flight possible some 300 to 400 years later.

The first of these four men was the Polish astronomer Nicolas Copernicus. In 1543 Copernicus published a new theory about the universe that corrected Ptolemy once and for all and put the other scientists back on the right track. Copernicus argued that the planets revolve around the sun, and he went on to point out that the earth rotates on its own axis around the sun once in every 24 hours.

Everyone knows this today. But it took courage in Copernicus' day to say it, especially since he was opposing what other experts had said and had no real way of proving he was correct. There was still no telescope—it would not be put into use until the early 1600's. And Copernicus did not

know enough about complex mathematics to make precise calculations on paper. He simply relied on logic.

The job of proving Copernicus correct with mathematics was left for the second of our four men, a German astronomer named Johannes Kepler, who lived from 1571 to 1630. Kepler formulated a series of mathematical laws which not only supported Copernicus but went on to add other ideas. He proved on paper, for example, that the earth and the other planets do not move around the sun in perfect circular orbits as everyone assumed, but in elliptical (egg-shaped) orbits that bring each planet closer to the sun at some points along its path and farther away at others. Kepler calculated the movements of the planets and the shape of their orbits so exactly that his equations are still used today, more than 300 years later, to help plot rocket flights into space. And one of the first things the American astro-

16

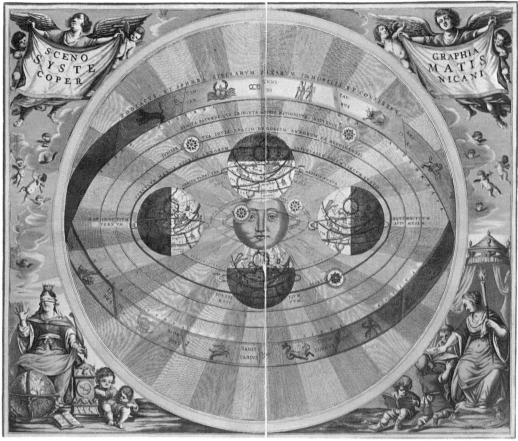

nauts had to do when they joined Project Mercury was review their college physics, including Kepler's laws.

By this time—the time when European seamen were competing with each other to reach the New World in force—the telescope had finally been invented. And the third scientist on our list was making good use of one of the first telescopes at his observatory in Italy. The man was Galileo Galilei —better known by his first name. His telescope was a tiny, fragile affair which he himself had perfected.

Though it was no match for the huge instruments used by astronomers today, it was effective enough to allow Galileo to begin making truly scientific observations and thus to give the study of space a vital leap forward.

Galileo was the first to discover, for example, that there are mountains on the moon. This immediately led other scientists to assume that the moon, being made of materials similar to the earth's, must therefore share with it common origins. He was also the first to notice that the planet Jupiter has

17

small moons of its own floating in orbit around it. This, in turn, led other scientists to realize that planets have gravitational fields that allow satellites to circle them without whisking off into space. And because Galileo was the first trained astronomer to have a close look at the universe, he was also the first scientist to arrive at some idea of the relative sizes of the various stars and planets and the tremendous distances that separate them from one another.

The fourth scientist who filled in much of our present knowledge of space was born in the same year that Galileo died—1642. He was the Eng-

David Rittenhouse of Philadelphia built the first American telescope (above) in 1769.

lish mathematician, Isaac Newton. It was Newton, more than any other man of his day, who prepared the way for our exploration of space three centuries later. His greatest contribution was a mathematical theory explaining the principle of earth's gravity. Newton got the idea, according to legend, when he sat under an apple tree one day and watched an apple falling to the ground. It was the earth's pull of gravity, Newton said, that caused objects like the apple to fall to earth, that also caused other objects on the earth's surface to cling to it, and that even caused the earth's moon to be held in its fixed orbit as it circled the earth.

It was only a short step from this basic discovery to Newton's next conclusion. If a falling object like an apple is pulled toward earth with a known speed and force, it would therefore require an equal speed and force to cancel out the pull of gravity and propel the object away from earth and into space. This was a momentous idea, and Newton even went so far as to calculate the exact speed required. After making many painstaking experiments, he decided that an object falling toward earth reaches a maximum speed of about 25,000 mph, or about 36,000 feet per second. Therefore, any object would have to reach that same tremendous speed—in the opposite direction—to get away from earth's grip and fly into space.

This finding of Newton's was enough to convince almost everyone in those days that it would be physi-

18

cally impossible for man to hurl objects from earth into space. In an age when the fastest known projectiles were musket and cannon balls that only went 1,100 feet per second, no serious scientist could even conceive of a device that could be made to go some thirty-three times that speed.

But if this one part of Newton's theories discouraged the scientists from even thinking about sending objects into space, another part of his findings—that the moon was one of the earth's satellites and was in the grip of earth's gravity—only increased public curiosity about space travel and whetted people's appetite for it. For when the idea began to get around that the moon circles the earth on a predictable path and is practically a cousin of the earth's, all kinds of adventurers began daydreaming about the possibility of going there.

One of the most famous of all daydreams about space travel was a book published in 1865 by the popular French writer of science fiction, Jules Verne. The book was titled *From the Earth to the Moon.* Verne also wrote exciting adventure stories about diving into the sea in a submarine (*Twenty Thousand Leagues Under the Sea*) and soaring along in a balloon (*Around the World in 80 Days*), and he tried to make his yarn about space as realistic as possible.

Verne made some mistakes, but he understood the principles of Isaac Newton. He had the characters in his story use a gigantic cannon 900 feet

America's early passion for space is illustrated by the scene decorating this mid nineteenth century hatbox. A telescope (right) is trained on an oversized moon (left), which is imaginatively covered with palm trees and peopled with strange winged moon creatures.

long to give their spacecraft the tremendous standing start he knew it would need to overcome the grip of gravity and get off the ground. Verne did not seem to realize that such a violent, explosive blast-off would kill the crew and passengers before they ever left the gun barrel. (The rockets that take men into space do not use a huge, one-shot explosion of energy to leave the ground. Instead there is a long, steady surge of power that begins slowly on the launching pad and builds up while the spacecraft rises until it reaches maximum speed just as the rocket tosses its cargo into orbit.)

But Verne did realize what would happen once his passengers left the pull of earth's gravity behind. Without gravity to hold them down or give them weight, they would be entirely weightless and would just float along. He was absolutely correct in his description of a poor dog that died early in the voyage and had to be thrown overboard. The dog weighed only a fraction of what the huge spaceship weighed, but the two objects went floating along side-by-side, and the passengers could look out and see the dog following them.

There was also a squawking chicken on board—for the chef to use when the menu called for it. (This was a first-class flight, complete with table-cloths.) Though Verne did not mention it, he could also have had one of his characters pluck a feather from the chicken and toss it overboard too. The feather, the dog, and the spacecraft would have floated together. For there is no difference in weight between objects that are weightless. Because all three objects were fired from the cannon together, they all had the same momentum and were traveling at the same speed.

Verne was almost prophetic in his choice of a launching pad. Though he was writing primarily for a European audience, he located the pad in southern Florida, not far from the present site of Cape Canaveral (now called Cape Kennedy), where the real astronauts began their flights less than a hundred years after Verne's.

Everyone knew that Jules Verne's story was pure fiction. But perhaps one reason it was such a great success was that many of its readers had a

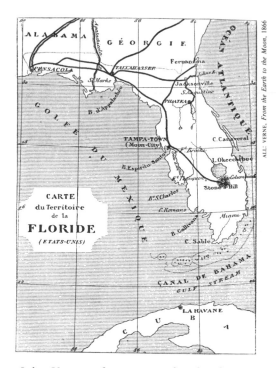

Jules Verne, after writing for the theatre, began to produce his famous science fiction tales in 1862. Without scientific training, and using only his imagination, he foretold many future events. From the Earth to the Moon, *first published in 1865, described a moon shot with uncanny accuracy. Verne*

20

chose a spot near Cape Canaveral (opposite, top) as the site of an underground cannon that hurled his multistage rocket (at bottom) into space. Above, his passengers enjoy the feeling of weightlessness, and below, the dog that died and was thrown overboard from the missile follows along at the same rate.

hunch the time would come when parts of the yarn, at least, might come true. Even some of the most hard-headed scientists were beginning to get more interested in space at this time. They had developed stronger telescopes in the late 1800's and early 1900's, and they were unraveling more secrets about the universe almost every day. But they still wanted to learn more. The best way for them to do this, of course, would be to go up into space themselves to take a closer look at some of the mysteries. They still could not think of a way to beat Newton's law of gravity and go zooming off into the depths of space. But they did have a new tool of exploration that could take them at least into the lower fringes of space. This vehicle was the lighter-than-air balloon that Jules Verne had also made the most of in *Around the World in 80 Days*.

In 1870 three Frenchmen led by a Professor Gaston Tissandier floated up to what was then the fantastic height of five miles. Their purpose was to disprove a belief held by other experts that the upper levels of air were so dangerous that man could not travel through them. The three pioneers came down safely from their record altitude, and man's knowledge of—and confidence in—space began to grow.

The balloon remained the scientists' best means of exploring space for a number of years. It could operate at a higher altitude than the most modern airplane—because even a jet plane needs a natural supply of oxygen to

21

The first manned balloon ascent (above) was made by Pilatre de Rozier and the Marquis d'Arlandes in 1783. Just over a year later, another Frenchman and an American, John Jeffries, crossed the English Channel in a balloon (right). Charles F. Durant (below), America's first balloonist, made an ascent from Castle Garden, New York, in 1830.

Union general George McClellan used a balloon on the James River to observe Confederate troops during his Peninsula campaign.

make the fuel burn to drive its engines, and also because an airplane must push against fairly heavy air in order to get support from its wings; a balloon, which has no wings, can go higher up where the air is thinner and there is very little oxygen.

In May, 1931, the Swiss physicist Auguste Piccard reached what was then a record balloon altitude of 51,793 feet. A year later he soared to more than 55,000 feet. Both of these flights were for scientific purposes: to measure and study cosmic rays, the mysterious carriers of explosive energy which bombard the earth—sometimes with deadly effect—from far out in space. In the last few years American balloonists have gone up even higher. Captain Joseph W. Kittinger, Jr. of the U.S. Air Force parachuted from a balloon at the record height of 102,800 feet on August 16, 1960, and helped a civilian astronomer reach the height of 81,000 feet on another flight. In 1961 Commanders Malcolm Ross and Victor Prather of the U.S. Navy soared together to an altitude of 21.5 miles, the highest ascent yet.

The purpose of all these flights was to pioneer and to gather scientific knowledge. Commander Prather—who unfortunately was killed in an accident as he was being fished out of the ocean after landing—was seeking medical data on the effects of high altitude flights on a man's body. Kittinger made his parachute jump to test man's ability to survive such a leap from the edge of space. The purpose of his flight with the astronomer William White was to get a trained observer and a telescope as high into the sky as possible to see if the stars still twinkled there.

This whimsical-sounding question is one of the major problems that have always bothered astronomers. By space observation it has been determined at last that the stars do not really twinkle out in space. They only seem to blink off and on for us here on earth because billions of tiny particles of dust floating around in the earth's atmosphere keep blocking out the light from the stars and make them seem to flicker off. For this rea-

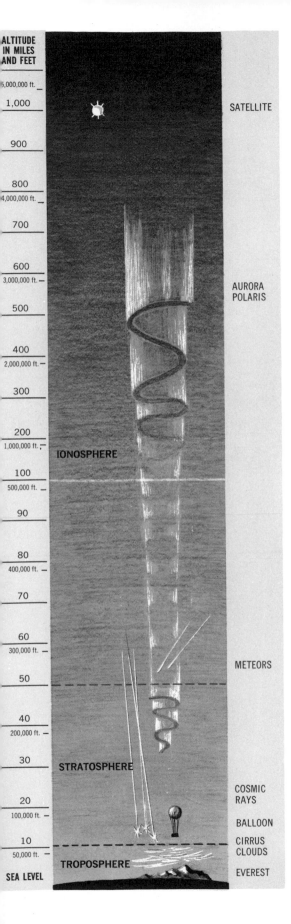

son, the astronomers are extremely anxious to get their telescopes and other instruments out beyond the earth's atmosphere where they can see the stars more clearly. The astronomers say that if they can only measure the stars' true light and the true heat that the stars give off, then they will be able to solve many of the mysteries about the age, distances, and structure of the universe.

But the astronomers are not the only scientists who are interested in going into space. The weather experts also want to make measurements far above the earth. If they can only spot the huge storms nearer their sources, the experts say that they can predict far ahead of time such expensive acts of nature as floods and drought that now cause untold damage each year to the nation's crops simply because there is no way of warning farmers that unusual weather patterns are on the way.

This, then, became the goal—to help scientific observers get out into space where they could increase man's knowledge about his environment and help him to cope with it. That was just a dream centuries ago, a subject only for adventure stories. Now it is slowly becoming a reality.

Space begins at the upper edge of the "sensible" atmosphere, fifty miles above the surface of the earth. Once considered a simple envelope of gas surrounding the planet, the atmosphere is now known to consist of a series of different layers (diagram at left).

25

Balloons still play their part in man's quest for the stars because they can take him higher than any other device not powered by rockets. The Strato Lab High-V balloon below, carrying Commanders Victor Prather and Malcolm Ross of the U.S. Navy, soared to a record height of 21.5 miles in 1961. From a similar balloon, U.S. Air Force captain Joseph W. Kittinger parachuted 102,800 feet to set the world's record. An automatic camera recorded his departure (right) and the first 3 seconds of his 13-minute 45-second drop to earth (sequence opposite).

The reality has been slow to come because scientists have learned only in recent years that a way might be developed to overcome earth's gravity and put trained observers and their instruments into space. Nor could the scientists do the job all by themselves. They needed the support of the public and their governments in order to raise the huge sums of money that are needed to explore and conquer space. The money and the public support have been as hard to come by in this century as were funds for exploration in the time of Columbus.

The United States was not the first country to recognize the value of space exploration and the possibility of carrying it out. A Russian, Konstantin Tsiolkovsky, had published a paper on the feasibility of space flight by rocket in 1898. And it was the Soviet Union that took the first big steps into space and set the pace in the next century. But the man who first demonstrated that space flight could be a reality was an American scientist who was born in 1882 (before the airplane was invented) and died in 1945 (twelve years before the space age began with the first Russian Sputnik). It was this American pioneer who devised and tested the mechanical means that the Russians—and later the Americans—used to get into space. In fact, he was so far ahead of his time that he patented his first ideas on how to reach space in 1914, years before John Glenn and the other astronauts had even been born. The scientist was 32 years old at the time, and his name was Robert Hutchings Goddard.

2

AMERICA'S PIONEER

It was behind the family farmhouse near Worcester, Massachusetts, that the idea first came to Robert Hutchings Goddard. He was only 17 at the time, and he had clambered up into a cherry tree to trim away some dead branches. But then he looked down at the fields beneath him and forgot about the branches and began thinking about something else. That something else was space.

The year was 1899, and he had just finished reading some recent books on space travel—one by Jules Verne and another about an interplanetary conflict called *The War of the Worlds* by the English writer H.G. Wells. As he looked down from the cherry tree, Goddard stopped trimming the dead branches and began to daydream. "I imagined how wonderful it would be," he later wrote in an autobiographical note, "to make some device which had even the *possibility* of ascending to

This tower was built in the 1930's at Eden Valley, New Mexico, by Robert H. Goddard, America's rocket pioneer; it was the first hint of Cape Kennedy's later gantries.

Mars, and how it would look on a small scale if sent up from the meadow at my feet."

Goddard climbed down from the tree with his life's work all laid out for him. He had not heard of anyone else who was thinking seriously about space exploration, so he decided he would have to tackle the job himself and make it his career. He even realized what kind of device he would need to send men into space. It would have to be a rocket.

It is amazing that Robert Goddard should have seized on this idea some 40 years before it was widely accepted even in academic circles. But he already understood enough from his high school physics to know the limitations of the balloon for space flight. (When a lighter-than-air craft rises to an altitude where the atmosphere becomes thin, the pressure inside the craft is equalized with the pressure outside, and the balloon can go no higher.) Young Goddard also had enough theoretical knowledge to see that any successful heavier-than-air craft could not fly in space if it used wings or an air-breathing engine.

Instead, he chose the rocket, a device that had often been used in the past. Though some of the nineteenth-century English rockets had carried hefty war heads and could cover a mile with their high, screaming trajectory, most of the early rockets were small, crude affairs. They could make a loud noise and a big flash but could not go much higher than a mile or so at the most. By the time Goddard was a boy, most nations had abandoned the rocket as a weapon. It was used only now and then as a distress signal or to fling a life line out to a sinking ship in the harbor. As far as the general public was concerned, the chief purpose of the rocket in Goddard's time was to make a spectacular show on the Fourth of July after everyone had eaten his watermelon.

It is a sign of Goddard's genius that he knew the rocket was capable of doing much more than that. He was convinced that it was chiefly a matter of making rockets both lighter and more powerful, and that this could be done by discovering a better fuel than the black powder which had been used until then. Goddard would also try to improve the workings of the rocket so it would be capable of carrying a valuable cargo into space without fizzling out. Then he would seek to perfect some kind of guidance system to keep it from veering off course as many rockets did.

Goddard had no illusions about how difficult it would be to do all of this. He realized that since no one else was studying or teaching the subject, he would have to learn the basic principles of rocketry by himself. He also realized that in order to make im-

provements in the fuels and controls, he would have to learn all there was to know about advanced chemistry, physics, and mathematics. There were no textbooks in this field; he would have to write the chapters himself as he went along.

Despite this enormous challenge, young Goddard was convinced he was on the right track. Fortunately, he understood the nature of the universe as described by Copernicus, Kepler, and Galileo. More importantly, he comprehended Isaac Newton's laws better than most college professors did—and he began to make use of them. One of Newton's findings that Goddard believed would help him find a solution to the problem of gravity was Newton's simple statement that "For each action there is an equal, and opposite, reaction."

In 1829, Lewis Miller of York, Pennsylvania, sketched two chemists whose experiment with rocket powder exploded (above). Two decades later, thirteen-year-old Winslow Homer drew his idea of a rocket ship (below).

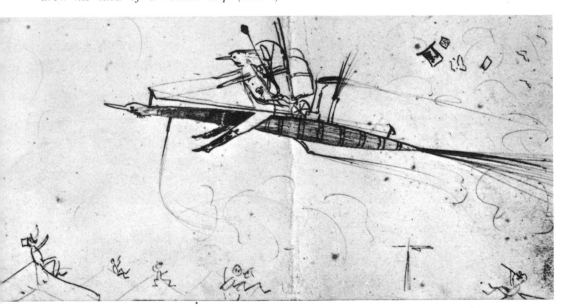

Perhaps the best example of Newton's brilliant theory is the modern rocket itself. It is almost as if Newton had the definition of a rocket in mind when he wrote the words down. For all rockets, whether they are small Fourth-of-July skyrockets or huge missiles like the Atlas, Titan, and Saturn, are based on the same principle. If you pack a container with energy in the form of fuel, and then exhaust this energy out the open rear end in the form of particles of hot gas given off by the burning fuel, the container will go zooming off in the opposite direction. The principle is as simple as that. The hot gas shooting out of the tail is the "action." The "opposite reaction" to this force is a similar thrust that pushes against the upper, or inside, wall of the rocket motor and makes the rocket soar off in the opposite direction. The height and speed that the rocket reaches will depend on how much energy has been packed into it.

All of this was clear in Goddard's mind from the very beginning. But he knew that although some first steps might be easy, others would be more difficult. For Goddard's driving ambition was to propel weighty objects into space along with the rockets themselves.

He realized that to keep probing higher and higher, it would be necessary to learn something more about the strange environment of space with each rocket shot. He would have to find some way to load his rockets with instruments to record data about conditions far above the earth's surface. Then, in order to study this data, he would have to equip rockets with some kind of parachute and recovery device to bring the recording instruments safely down again. He recognized, of course, that this paraphernalia would add considerable weight to the rocket and would call for even stronger fuel to get the whole package off the ground.

But he went to work experimenting with one idea after another. It was slow going. Twenty-seven years passed between the time Goddard climbed down from the cherry tree and the time when he was ready to test-fire his first rocket. And during this interval, while he was a student, there were many setbacks. In 1913, after graduating from college and going on to study more advanced physics, he became seriously

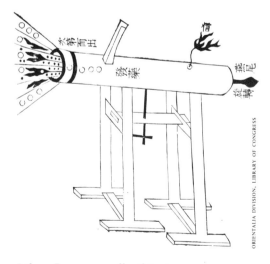

ORIENTALIA DIVISION, LIBRARY OF CONGRESS

Like a Roman candle, this sixteenth-century Chinese rocket only made a show of "action."

32

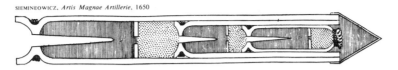

SIEMINEOWICZ, *Artis Magnae Artillerie*, 1650

This rocket made good use of the "reaction" caused when three successive powder charges exploded from its tail: it shot ahead with sustained thrust. It was designed by Casimir Siemineowicz in 1650.

ill with tuberculosis. At one point, the doctors gave him only two weeks to live. But the indomitable Goddard fooled them. "I felt I had to stay alive to complete my work," he said.

Also in 1913, though he was still so weak he could hardly hold his pen, he methodically wrote down in his notebooks the basic ideas of rocketry that were to form the outline for most of his future work. In 1914, though he still had not tested out a single rocket on a launching platform, Goddard was so sure of his theories that he took out two U.S. government patents to cover them. These were the first of some 214 patents that Goddard was to be granted during and after his lifetime. Altogether, they covered the science of rocketry so thoroughly that it is almost impossible to design or build a rocket today without relying in some way on these original inventions of Robert Goddard.

Except for the information that he had to reveal in order to get his patents, Goddard carefully kept most of his ideas to himself. He realized that U.S. government patents are available to anyone who asks for them, and he seemed to feel that it might be

dangerous for the United States if too many of his detailed ideas found their way to foreign countries like Germany and Russia where someone might make warlike use of them.

But Goddard, who was earning his living as a physics professor at Clark University in Worcester, Massachusetts, also realized that he needed financial support to pay for all of the expensive materials and special equipment involved in rocket research. In 1916, therefore, he wrote a scientific treatise that summarized his ideas and sent it to various institutions that might be interested in supporting him. Later, in 1919, it was published by the Smithsonian Institution in Washington, D.C.

The paper was basically a dry document full of equations and scientific jargon. But Goddard, a shy man who tried to avoid making fantastic predictions, also mentioned casually in his paper that it was mathematically possible for a rocket from the earth to reach the moon. When his paper was made public, the newspapers immediately singled out this one item about a flight to the moon and ignored most of the rest. From then on, one of

Robert Goddard's biggest problems was overcoming the idea, which many people had, that he was some kind of crackpot who thought he could hit the moon.

Just as Goddard suspected, his ideas did interest scientists here and abroad. And it was the Germans, under the leadership of Hermann Oberth, who started making greater strides in rocket research than Goddard's own nation. He found very little support for his work in the United States.

However, in 1917 the Smithsonian Institution granted him $5,000, a large sum in those days. This was enough to help Goddard equip a modest laboratory and hire two trained assistants. But he still had to spend so much of his time teaching physics in order to support himself, that he could devote only late afternoons, holidays, and summer vacations to his research.

This was the main reason that it took Goddard so long to perfect his ideas. It was not until March 16, 1926,

During the War of 1812, rockets were used as weapons by the British both on land and at sea. Rockets mounted on the masts of the fireships above

that Robert Goddard was finally ready to leave the laboratory and try firing his first rocket out of doors. The event took place on his Aunt Effie's farm near Auburn, Massachusetts. (The site is now a golf course.) And though the rocket was a crude contraption only 10 feet high, it was a direct ancestor of nearly every rocket that has been launched anywhere since then. (See photographs on pages 40 and 41.)

The propellant to make it go was a mixture of gasoline and liquid oxygen —almost the same combination that the Germans used in their V-2s some 18 years later and that the Americans were still using to put astronauts into orbit nearly 20 years after that. The gasoline served as the fuel—giving off the hot gas that provided the "action." As the rocket engine started, the liquid oxygen was mixed with the gasoline in order to make the flame even hotter for extra power, and also to provide oxygen to keep the gasoline burning once the rocket got so high in the at-

were ignited by flames that crept up the rigging as the British vessels were
sent down on the American fleet anchored off Fort McHenry, Maryland.

mosphere that there was no oxygen.

Goddard had only two assistants on his Aunt Effie's farm that day, a machinist named Henry Sachs who helped him set up the rocket inside its launching frame, and a young physics instructor, Dr. P. M. Roope, who measured the flight. The frame itself was a crude affair that looked more like a climbing rig on a children's playground than a device for space flight. And the rocket it held looked rather crude, too. But it was extremely well designed, and Goddard had already figured out some neat tricks to make it work with maximum efficiency.

He knew, for example, that it was necessary to keep the oxygen supply under the correct pressure so that the oxidizer would flow evenly into the combustion chamber and mix with the fuel in the correct proportion. If either liquid flowed in too fast at the start, there would not be enough of it left over at the end to complete the flight. On the other hand, if the liquids flowed too slowly, the mixture might not burn hotly enough to give off the required energy.

To make sure of an even flow, Goddard drilled the holes that the two liquids would flow through with great precision so they would mix just the way he wanted them to. He did not want a huge explosion that would only damage the rocket and burn up all of the fuel at once. Instead, he needed a carefully controlled combustion that would be powerful enough at the start simply to lift the rocket off the ground

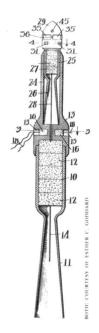

Two of Goddard's most important contributions were his multi-stage rocket design of 1914 (above) and his research into liquid fuels, with which he was occupied as early as May, 1910, the date of the journal opposite.

and give it an initial push. After that, he counted on other things happening to keep the rocket going.

For one thing, as the rocket expended some of its fuel it would get lighter—and this would help it go faster. The rocket would start moving even faster if it could keep working until it reached an altitude where the air got so thin that the rocket had less and less resistance to push against. Goddard felt that if he could only make a rocket work at maximum efficiency up to this point, he might achieve a combination of forces that

36

Suggestions of ways of
using the Jet - Solar energy Props.

1. Jet. (a) Have liquid fuel lead into an impulsive combustion chamber. C, (of course it would have to be forced in, using H_2O or gasoline + N_2O_5.

(b) The same, except the pressure is developed (allowed) all through the chamber. (necessitates stronger walls.

(c) An explosive, eg smokeless powder, taken as the, or arranged so as to be, slow burning (Selep) compressed. (if too rapid, use forcing.

× (Test this with telescope pointed towards the sun, in daytime - the shells being painted black.

(Also try with fuel, imbued with springs, ...)

(d) Remember, the next tier must be set off when the pressure has fallen.

× bring this grit the next smaller shell fitting into it.

× (1) Have ... crude gauges ignite upper tier, when all have been lowered.

(e) Of course means must be had to prevent dangerous explosion if a molten penetrates. Have in H_2O, a wall ..., send the heat, by igniter at hole if swells up the spring.

Have such a miniature in ... that ... a thing will not explode, ...

2. Application of Solar energy.
  1. Heat the jet
  2. Electrify the jet
  3. Heat other mass
  4. Electrify ...
  5. Perhaps have the extra mass as $H + O_2$? introduce these into the steam boiler (turbine) as previously described, thus previously ... heat.

(1. may be illustrated as — ... heat the jet directly.

(In the case of $2 ÷ 4$, the boiler (...) turbine + generator could be used.

- The reflectors had best be arranged as follows. ... each ready its sun up, by a separate, smaller mirror. This arrangement is ... economize. & the heavy support necessary if the mirror is all in one piece.

(In the case of one, each shell might have its own mirror.

$3 ÷ 4$. Have matter electrically sent off, after being exploded, at the focus of a paraboloid; the surface of which is charged.

---

would give him the terrific power and speed he was after. He was on the right track; this was the basic principle of rocketry that the space engineers would be striving to perfect for years to come.

That morning at Aunt Effie's farm, however, the scene was a far cry from the big, sleek launching pads at Cape Kennedy. Using a gasoline blowtorch tied to a stick, Goddard's assistant Henry Sachs lighted the igniter on the rocket that would later be used to start the fuel burning. When the igniter started putting out black smoke, indicating that it was burning properly, Sachs also lighted a small alcohol stove under the tank of liquid oxygen to help get the oxygen to the correct pressure. At this point, Goddard opened the valve on an oxygen cylinder 30 feet from the lauching frame to send a stream of oxygen gas into the rocket to build up the pressure even more. Finally, when everything was set, there was a rush of flame, and the rocket whooshed out of its framework with a roar. It rose to an altitude of about 40 feet and reached a speed of about 60 mph. Then two and one-

half seconds after lift-off, the rocket fell back to earth 184 feet from where it had started.

This was obviously only a modest beginning, but Goddard was pleased. He had been working with a very tricky combination of liquids that had never been used before, and he felt he was fortunate that they behaved the way he wanted them to and did not blow up. (The mixture of gasoline and liquid oxygen is five times as powerful as an equal weight of TNT.) All that Goddard had to do now, he told himself, was improve the plumbing, perfect the fuel mixture, and gradually increase the size of his rockets until he could achieve higher altitudes.

Goddard had three more flights at his Aunt Effie's farm. The last one was fired off on a July day in 1929, and it got Robert Goddard into deep trouble. This fourth rocket was more complicated than the first three. It had a camera, a thermometer, and a barometer tucked under the fuel tanks to record flight data. And Goddard had high hopes for the experiment. Unfortunately, it was a very quiet day around Auburn—the kind of still, summer day when sound carries a long way. The rocket soared up to a height of 90 feet. Then it nosed over prematurely and shot along for 171 feet

Robert H. Goddard's portrait (left) shows him in the robes of a Doctor of Science of Clark University, where he taught physics (right) and began space-flight experiments.

on a horizontal path before it plummeted back to earth and broke apart.

Because of the quiet day, quite a few people heard the noise of the take-off and were looking in the direction of Aunt Effie's farm when the rocket nosed over and fell. They had no idea what it was, but somebody must have seen the flame licking out of the rocket exhaust and called the police and fire departments to report that an airplane had crashed in flames. The police, a fire truck, two ambulances, and some newspaper reporters all came running.

No one was hurt, and Goddard begged the reporters to forget the incident. He knew the publicity would make it difficult for him to work quietly, the way he wanted to. But the newspaper stories came out anyway, and some of them continued to promote the idea that Dr. Goddard was a screwball scientist who was trying to

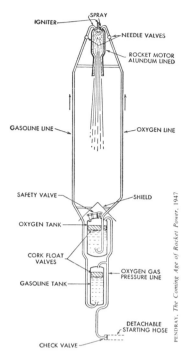

Labels (diagram): IGNITER, SPRAY, NEEDLE VALVES, ROCKET MOTOR ALUNDUM LINED, GASOLINE LINE, OXYGEN LINE, SAFETY VALVE, SHIELD, OXYGEN TANK, CORK FLOAT VALVES, OXYGEN GAS PRESSURE LINE, GASOLINE TANK, DETACHABLE STARTING HOSE, CHECK VALVE

PENDRAY, *The Coming Age of Rocket Power,* 1947

Goddard's liquid-fuel rocket (opposite) had to be ignited by hand. The fuel tanks (at bottom in the designer's own drawing above) were connected with the combustion chamber by feed lines that also served as a rigid frame for the rocket. The first successful firing took place in March, 1926, at his aunt's farm (above, left) in Massachusetts.

get to the moon. One sarcastic headline read: "MOON ROCKET MISSES TARGET BY 238,799-1/2 MILES."

The public ridicule was bad enough. But the reaction of a few local officials gave Goddard even more trouble. Within a few weeks the Massachusetts fire marshal ruled that Goddard had to stop his experiments on the farm in the interests of public safety.

Fortunately there were serious students of flight who were alarmed at the restrictions being put on Goddard. The U.S. Government accordingly came to the rescue and gave Goddard permission to fire his rockets from an army artillery range at Camp Devens, 25 miles away. But, like all

rocket men who have followed him, Goddard needed ideal conditions for his tests. He soon learned that by the time he could load up his equipment at home and drive it over bumpy roads all the way to Camp Devens, either the insides of the rockets would be shaken up or the fickle New England weather would suddenly change on him and stop the test.

It was just at this point that Dr.

41

Goddard had a great piece of luck. *The New York Times* had run a story about his July flight. And though many people missed seeing it on the inside pages, one man who read the story was Charles A. Lindbergh, the "Lone Eagle," who had startled the world just two years before when he flew alone and nonstop from New York to Paris in the *Spirit of St. Louis.*

Lindbergh was intrigued by the news that a learned scientist was engaged in serious work with rockets. A thoughtful student of aviation, Lindbergh had also come to the conclusion that the airplane was limited in speed and altitude capability, and that the real future of aviation depended on the development of rocket power. The Lone Eagle had even talked to some leading engineers about the subject. They all assured him the idea was impossible. But Lindbergh was not convinced; he decided to see Goddard.

The spectacular launching of July, 1929, was photographed by Esther Goddard, who kept a film record of her husband's experiments for later study. Above, the rocket is ready in the tower, which was needed to keep it vertical in the crucial first seconds of flight. Below, a sequence of frames from the motion picture of the launching show the rocket escaping from the tower on its historic trip.

The visit took place in November, 1929, in Goddard's office at Clark University. Lindbergh came away from the meeting convinced that Dr. Goddard deserved a chance to test out his theories. He left the professor with a promise that he would try to use his own prestige and influence to find financial backing for him.

Several months went by before Lindbergh could keep his promise. But he lined up support for Goddard from Daniel Guggenheim, a wealthy copper manufacturer whom Lindbergh knew, who agreed to contribute $25,000 a year to Goddard for a period of two years. This was a sum that Goddard himself suggested. It would free him of his teaching chores, enable him to purchase more materials, hire more help, and run more tests. It would also allow him to move his experiments out of Massachusetts.

Goddard picked a small ranch out-side Roswell, New Mexico, for his site. Here he felt he would have the privacy he required to concentrate on his studies, and also the clear, dry air and level terrain his rockets would need in order to work best. With the help of four assistants, Goddard erected a 60-foot launching tower at a location called Eden Valley. Then he built a shed a thousand feet away for his first control shelter and went to work. Two of his early but minor problems at the site were keeping the hawks from making nests in the launching tower and trying to keep scorpions and rattlesnakes from slipping into the control shack.

Despite these complications, Goddard got off to a good start. The first rocket he fired in New Mexico—in December, 1930—went up to an altitude of 2,000 feet and reached a top speed of 500 mph, which was a record at that time for any kind of engine.

Goddard was eager to make improvements on each rocket before he fired off the next one. He wanted to develop a better stabilizer, for example, to keep the rocket on a steady course as it went up. He needed an improved parachute release to make sure he got his rockets back in one piece so he could study them. And to help keep the combustion chamber from getting so hot it might burn through and ruin a flight, he tried to devise a better cooling system inside and around the rocket engine.

Even with four assistants to help him, this was slow, painstaking work. The special materials and parts that Goddard needed were so expensive to make—most of them had to be hand-tooled—that he used them over and over again if they were not damaged in a flight.

Mrs. Goddard, a cheerful, dedicated lady whom the professor had met and married back at Clark University, helped her husband with much of his work. She typed his notes on all the experiments and made movies of each test so Dr. Goddard could study them afterwards to see how well the rocket had performed. One day he showed some of this film to the Roswell Rotary Club to help explain to his friends and neighbors what he was up to. In one sequence a rocket nosed over and started veering back towards the camera. "The rascal tried to get me," Goddard said with a smile.

It was a fortunate thing for the future of space flight that Robert Goddard had a good sense of humor, a tremendous store of patience, and a way of not letting disappointments upset him. For there were a lot of failures to come. The desert weather sometimes proved to be just as cranky as New England weather, and on some occasions a rocket test was canceled by a sudden dust storm charging across the prairie. But in March, 1935, Goddard had an especially successful

In 1940 Goddard successfully launched a 22-foot turbo-pump rocket (opposite) that represented a great advance over earlier rockets. Its construction was aided by Harry F. Guggenheim and Charles A. Lindbergh (on either side of Goddard in the picture at left).

At Eden Valley, Goddard pushed ahead with his work. At left, he supervises the final assembly of a rocket, which was carried to the launching site on a special trailer (below). From the control shack (bottom) one thousand feet from the launching tower, he views the gauges through a telescope while his hand rests on the three-button control panel. Opposite, a Goddard rocket leaves a trail of smoke as it hurtles into the sky.

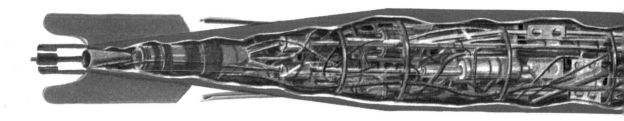

flight when a rocket reached a speed of nearly 750 mph, the speed of sound. In May, 1935, another of Goddard's rockets climbed to an altitude of 7,500 feet while correcting itself to vertical flight—"like a fish swimming upward," his wife remarked.

Goddard felt so encouraged by these and other successes he decided to invite Lindbergh and his sponsor, Harry F. Guggenheim (son of the philanthropist Daniel Guggenheim), out to the ranch to watch the next rocket test. The two men accepted and flew to Roswell in Lindbergh's plane. On the morning of September 22, 1935, they went out in the cold dawn to the small control shelter, and when everything was ready and all the last-minute adjustments were made, Goddard pressed the "GO" button on his control panel. But nothing happened. The rocket just sat there. Goddard had a stand-by rocket ready for just such an emergency, but before he could get it set up for firing, a desert cloudburst let loose and soaked all the equipment. In a small way, Goddard was going through the same headaches that so often plagued the technicians

Goddard's 1941 design became the model for many future rockets. The nose cone (colored yellow in the drawing above) carried a recovery parachute. The gasoline fuel tank (green) was mounted immediately behind it, and the liquid-oxygen tank (also green) was near the center. The steering gyroscope (blue) was between them. Two pumps (yellow) fed the fuel mixture to the combustion chamber (salmon) in the tail. The air vanes (blue) and tail fins (orange) stabilized the flight.

at Cape Kennedy many years later.

There was one more bad day for Goddard before his guests had to leave. He tried a final time to fire one of his rockets so his financial backers could get a more accurate idea of what it could do. This time, a bright flame appeared from the combustion chamber. But the rocket itself refused to budge. Goddard decided from the noise and the color of the flame—he was an expert in these details by now—that there was too much oxygen in the mixture. He was terribly embarrassed. But his two sponsors assured Goddard that they had faith in him, and that they understood how easy it was for things to go wrong in the early stages of such a complicated program. When they took off in Lindbergh's

plane, the Lone Eagle dipped his wings over Goddard's ranch in an aviator's salute from one pioneer to another.

Two more years went by, years of tinkering and improvement. The rocket was becoming a much more complex and smoother-running piece of machinery by now. Goddard figured out ways to cool the engine that were simple and logical—a cooling jacket was put around the combustion chamber, and the fuel was pumped through this on its way to being ignited. He developed a device—ten years before the Germans did—to keep a rocket steady in flight with guidance vanes, electrically controlled by a gyroscope.

He was the first to try out the idea of steering a rocket by placing metal vanes right in the blast of the engine and moving them back and forth to make the rocket change direction. He also steered the rocket by swiveling, or "gimbaling," the rocket motor itself back and forth—much as you keep a broomstick balanced in the air by moving your hand back and forth underneath it. Many of these ideas thought up by Goddard are standard procedure in rocket engineering today.

With so many new gadgets squeezed inside it, Goddard's rocket was also a good deal larger now than the ones he had started out with. On March 26, 1937, Goddard launched a rocket from the tower that was almost 16-1/2 feet high. It worked beautifully. The engine kept burning for 22 seconds after lift-off and carried the rocket to a record altitude of nearly 9,000 feet. Both Guggenheim and Lindbergh were extremely pleased when they heard the news. And the latter wrote Goddard from Europe that "I believe you are very close to the successful conclusion of what I consider the first stage of the project—that is, the development of a rocket that can attain higher altitudes than those reached by . . . balloons."

In 1940, after World War II had begun in Europe, Dr. Goddard was sure that the Germans were up to something in the way of rocketry. And he knew that his patents had been sent all over the world under the normal international exchange and were available to everyone. Because of this conviction, Goddard offered to make his own research available to the U.S.

military, so that his own nation could be prepared for whatever new weapons might appear. The American generals listened politely to Goddard's ideas, but they turned him down.

At this moment, the government of Nazi Germany had 12,000 rocket technicians working full time to prepare their dreaded V-2 rockets. The V-2 was a missile that could soar to an altitude of 100 miles, then travel some 200–300 more miles at a speed of almost 1,800 mph to swoop down on enemy cities. London, England, would soon feel the full brunt of these awful weapons. In the United States, at this same time, Dr. Goddard was assigned by the Navy Department to work on a jet-assisted take-off device (JATO) using liquid propellants to help get airplanes off the ground.

But in a strange way Goddard's pioneering rocket work did help the United States win World War II. For during World War I, he had devised a rocket for the Army Signal Corps. The same invention was improved during World War II and used against German tanks. It was called the "bazooka."

Robert Goddard died in August, 1945. Just a few months before, he had gone with one of his assistants to inspect a German V-2 that had been captured intact and flown to the United States for inspection. As the American technicians pried open the world's first mass-produced, liquid-fueled rocket to see what it looked like inside, someone remarked that it was almost a carbon copy of the rocket

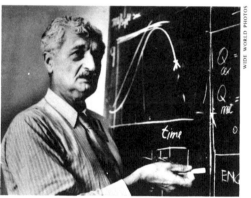

In developing the dreaded V-2 rockets (opposite) that were turned on England at the end of World War II, Germany used a huge force of men and a budget many thousand times larger than Goddard's. He, like the Russian rocket pioneer, self-educated theorist Konstantin Tsiolkovsky (top), worked mostly alone and in secrecy. Several German experts such as Hermann Oberth (above) later came to America to lend their talents to the space programs of the United States.

Dr. Goddard had been working on for years. Goddard took a good look at the German rocket and agreed. "It seems to be," he said modestly.

A few months after Goddard's death, the U.S. Army rounded up a number of German rocket engineers and brought them to the United States to help teach American engineers how to build rockets. The Germans readily admitted that though much of their learning had come from extensive experimentation and from attention to the ideas of scientists from other countries—notably Russia's Tsiolkovsky—an important boost to their work had been given by an American. In fact, Dr. Wernher von Braun, the leader of the German rocket team in the United States, who has since done so much to promote the U.S. space program, referred to Dr. Goddard as "my boyhood hero."

Many years after Goddard's death, the U.S. Government finally realized that the Atlases, Redstones, Thors, Polarises, and other rockets it had started to build were all based on Dr. Goddard's patents. It awarded Mrs. Goddard and the Daniel and Florence Guggenheim Foundation that had financed his early work the sum of one million dollars as a token of America's debt to a great pioneer.

Пролетарии всех стран, соединяйтесь!

Коммунистическая партия Советского Союза

ПРАВДА

Орган Центрального Комитета Коммунистической партии Советского Союза

Год издания 46-й · № 279 (14308) · Воскресенье, 6 октября 1957 года · ЦЕНА 30 КОП.

4 октября 1957 года в нашей стране произведён успешный запуск первого в мире искусственного спутника Земли. Спутник имеет форму шара диаметром 58 сантиметров и весом 83,6 килограмма.

В настоящее время спутник со скоростью около 8.000 метров в секунду описывает эллиптические траектории вокруг Земли.

За полётом спутника с огромным вниманием следят во всех странах мира.

Прогрессивное человечество горячо приветствует новую историческую победу Советского Союза в развитии науки и техники.

Первый в мире искусственный спутник Земли создан в Советской стране!

ТРИУМФ СОВЕТСКОЙ НАУКИ И ТЕХНИКИ

Самые дерзновенные мечты человечества становятся реальностью

Разведчикам небесных глубин

*Слава разведчикам небесных глубин
Слава науке
Слава КПСС*

Сергей ВАСИЛЬЕВ

Вершина науки

Фёдор ПАНФЁРОВ

Неоценимый вклад

Тодор ПАВЛОВ
Президент Болгарской академии наук.
г. София, 5 октября.

Радиолюбители с большим интересом следят за радиосигналами, получаемыми с искусственного спутника Земли. Вчера, 5 октября, в Ленинградском городском радиоклубе ДОСААФ с утра проходила дежурства радиолюбителей. Приём радиосигналов проводился. На приёме сигналов искусственного спутника Земли.
Фото М. Карасёва. (Снимок принят по фототелеграфу.)

О движении искусственного спутника Земли

С момента продолжения спутника Земли в районе Москвы в 1 час 46 минут 5 октября и до 10 часов 6 октября он сделает около 18 оборотов вокруг Земли.

5 октября

Гуалькаю — 17 часов 41 минута	Карачи — 20 часов 54 минуты
Мадрас — 17 часов 52 минуты	Алма-Ата — 20 часов 58 минут
Калькутта — 19 часов 12 минут	Багдад — 22 часа 32 минуты
Улан-Батор — 19 часов 22 минуты	

6 октября

Якутск — 0 часов 25 минут	Ленинград — 6 часов 49 минут
Рига — 1 час 41 минута	Москва — 8 часов 34 минуты
Рим — 1 час 52 минуты	Москва — 8 часов 34 минуты
Москва — 1 час 52 минуты	
Рангун — 5 часов 5 минут	Рим — 10 часов 9 минут
Бандунг — 5 часов 24 минуты	

5 октября

Галифакс — 16 часов 9 минут	Вашингтон — 16 часов 31 минута
Детройт — 16 часов 30 минут	

Будущее стало днём сегодняшним

Б. АРБУЗОВ
Академик.
г. Казань.

ЗАМЕЧАТЕЛЬНО!

Т. САРЫМСАКОВ
Ректор Средне-Азиатского государственного университета Академии наук Узбекской ССР.

В Москву проездом на родину из КНР прибыла Правительственная делегация Венгерской Народной Республики

(ТАСС).

Обед в Кремле в честь Правительственной делегации Венгерской Народной Республики

(ТАСС).

Приём Н. С. Хрущёвым делегации Союза борцов народно-освободительной войны Югославии

(ТАСС).

ТЕЛЕГРАММА

Товарищу Клименту Ефремовичу ВОРОШИЛОВУ Председателю Президиума Верховного Совета СССР

МОСКВА

Георгий ДАМЯНОВ
Председатель Президиума Народного собрания Народной Республики Болгарии.
г. София.

«Они сделали это первыми»

Заявление американского учёного д-ра Джозефа КАПЛАН

НЬЮ-ЙОРК, 5 октября. (ТАСС).

Мнение английского учёного

ЛОНДОН, 5 октября. (ТАСС).

Большая победа

Профессор Павел Ян НОВАЦКИЙ
Член-корреспондент Польской академии наук.

3

THE RACE BEGINS

On the fourth of October, 1957, Robert Goddard's worries and suspicions about rocket progress in certain foreign countries came true. For out of the Soviet Union on that day came the electrifying report that Soviet technicians had launched their first Sputnik —or satellite. With sensitive tracking equipment scientists throughout the world soon picked up the beeps of the satellite out in space and confirmed that the Russians had done exactly what they said they had done. They had put a satellite into orbit around the earth.

Sputnik I was only 22 inches. in diameter, and it weighed only 184 pounds. But it was destined to stay in orbit for three months, and the sudden surprise made U.S. scientists sit up and worry. For they had no plans on the boards to do anything as impressive as the Soviet achievement.

The orbit of the Soviet Union's Sputnik I, the first man-made satellite to circle the earth, is announced in Pravda *on October 6, 1957—two days after the launch. "Sputnik" is the fifth word in the main headline.*

In fact, just a month before the Russians launched their first Sputnik into orbit, civilian rocket engineers working for the U.S. government had suffered a serious setback at Cape Kennedy. They had tried to launch a test model of their mightiest rocket— an Atlas ICBM (Intercontinental Ballistic Missile) which, in the event of a war, would be capable of carrying a nuclear war head from a base in the United States to an enemy target thousands of miles away. Though many other smaller U.S. rockets had been successfully launched, and though an Army Redstone missile had been sent into space in 1953, this was the second time the mighty Atlas had failed in two tries. (In both cases, the rocket either blew up accidentally or had to be exploded on purpose to keep it from falling back on a populated area and doing a lot of damage.)

The rocket engineers were naturally very disappointed. They were even more discouraged when Sputnik I was sent up a month later—proving that the Russians were having much greater success with their rockets. And a month after that, when the

This U.S. rocket, the Redstone, was lobbed 680 miles into space; the nose cone was recovered 3,300 miles down range. But that record feat of 1956 was eclipsed by the orbiting of the Sputniks.

Russians put up their *second* Sputnik, Americans everywhere were bitterly disheartened. For this time, the Soviet satellite weighed over a thousand pounds, and inside, it carried a living passenger, a dog named Laika.

Laika did not survive the trip. She died painlessly when the oxygen in the capsule ran out, and both the dog and her capsule burned to a crisp as they re-entered the atmosphere on their way back to earth. Nevertheless, the event was so spectacular that it helped to change the minds of most Americans about space almost overnight. It was obvious now that if the Russians were so far advanced in rocketry that they could orbit a dog and keep it alive—at least until re-entry—in a capsule weighing half a ton, it was only a matter of time before they could top this feat themselves and send up even heavier satellites—perhaps with human passengers.

Most Americans agreed that something had to be done. A potential enemy that had usually been considered inferior to the United States in technology was suddenly playing a game of leapfrog and jumping right into the next century ahead of the U.S. America's prestige was at stake. Even more important than that was the dangerous possibility that unless the United States tried to catch up, the Soviet Union might find some way to use her new rocket power as a weapon to threaten American safety.

The big question was *how* to catch up. How could the United States, which had started to develop rockets after the Russians, manage to meet the Russian challenge and begin sending heavy objects into space—even small objects? Most American rocket experts had not been planning on using their rockets for space exploration. The American rockets—like the Atlas, Titan, and Corporal missiles—had been designed chiefly as defensive weapons. And since many of these early rockets were relatively small, short-range models, none of them was powerful enough to put a very heavy object into orbit anyway.

There was one man in the United States who wanted to try. He was Dr. Wernher von Braun, the brilliant scientist who had begun working with rockets in Berlin when he was a teenager. Von Braun was one of several German rocket experts who had surrendered to the U.S. Army during

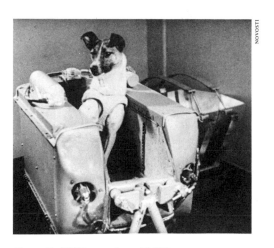

Sputnik II (November, 1957) was even more impressive than Sputnik I: it carried instruments and a dog-in-space named Laika.

World War II and had come to the United States to resume their careers. As soon as he arrived in America, Dr. von Braun began thinking up ways to help his new country catch up in rocket technique and space exploration. One product of Dr. von Braun's team of scientists was the U.S. Army Redstone, the 1500-mile intermediate-range missile that was destined to be used—several years later—to send the first American astronaut, Alan Shepard, on a short ballistic ride into space. Dr. von Braun was so confident of the accuracy and dependability of his Redstone that he suggested to U.S. authorities—three years before the first Soviet Sputnik—that a Redstone rocket could be used to put a small satellite into orbit around the earth. He explained that it would have to be a tiny one—the Redstone was not powerful enough to do anything more. But the authorities decided against the idea. Their reason was that the Redstone was primarily a military rocket, and they did not want to give the impression to the rest of the world that the United States was simply showing off its armed might.

The same philosophy still applied three years later when Sputnik I was launched in Russia. The United States was more anxious than ever to catch up in the space-exploration competition, but not at the risk of being criticized for using a military weapon to carry out a peaceful mission. In the meantime, as a way of getting around this problem—since most American rockets had been designed and produced for military purposes—American space officials had started to develop a purely "scientific" rocket called Vanguard. The designers of the Vanguard rocket had to start from scratch to avoid using military equipment, and the rocket therefore had to go through the same long, painstaking routine of testing and retesting that all other rockets had had to undergo from the time of Robert Goddard. This took so much time that it was not until the morning of December 6, 1957 —two months after Sputnik I—that the first Vanguard sat on its pad at Cape Kennedy with a would-be satellite poised on its nose. Late or not, the American space program was ready to begin.

The U.S. Government decided to handle the launching in a much different manner from the way in which the Russians had handled theirs. The Soviet Union launched all of its space experiments in complete secrecy and never announced them to the world until it was almost certain that they were successful. In order to dramatize the fact that the United States is a free society where such important events take place out in the open, it was decided to launch the Vanguard in full view of the press and foreign observers —for all the world to see. This was a brave but costly gamble. For at 11:46 o'clock on that December morning, the first Vanguard rocket blew up on the launching pad in a fierce ball of smoke and flame. The little satellite fell to the ground from the top of the rocket and just lay there, its radio beeping away pathetically.

Three months later, a second Vanguard rocket went up successfully. The satellite it put into orbit was so tiny—it weighed three pounds, four ounces, and was only 6.4 inches in diameter—that Russia's Premier Nikita Khrushchev dismissed it as a "grapefruit." Khrushchev smiled when he said this, however, and he should have. For though the Vanguard satellite was smaller than anything the Russians had launched, it could perform scientific feats that the Soviet satellites

The master of rockets, Wernher von Braun, lounges at his desk in Huntsville, Alabama. Behind him are models of U.S. rockets he helped develop. Third from left is the Redstone; two beyond that is a Redstone topped by America's first space capsule; the mighty Saturn V pokes through the ceiling.

*The first rocket from Cape Kennedy—then called Cape Canaveral
—was a German V-2 launched in 1950 (above). The site was se-
lected for its convenience to a new test range over the Atlantic.*

could not (see pages 60 and 65).

Vanguard was an excellent example of the way in which American technicians were learning to make the most of what they had to work with. Actually, it was far more difficult to construct a tiny satellite than a large one because all of the parts had to be much more intricate and more carefully made. There was no room in the tiny Vanguard satellite, for example, for conventional storage batteries to provide power for its radio and instruments. So the scientists outfitted it with solar cells that could recharge themselves over and over from the bright light of the sun to keep Vanguard working. Also, Vanguard was

58

put into such a perfect orbit that the scientists estimated it would remain in space for 2,000 years instead of just a few months, as the first Soviet satellites had.

In between the two Vanguard launchings—just after the failure and shortly before the final success—the United States launched another clever satellite that a group of engineers working with Dr. von Braun had been getting ready in the meantime. This was Explorer I, the first of a series of experiments designed to make a detailed scientific study of space. Explorer I was a cylinder 80 inches long and 6 inches in diameter. And it weighed only 31 pounds, 18 of which consisted of an incredibly complicated set of tiny instruments.

These instruments made an important discovery that none of the huge Soviet satellites had noticed. Explorer I sent back by radio the first solid evidence that much of the earth is covered by a series of thick belts of radiation. The belts were named for Dr. James Van Allen, the professor of physics at the University of Iowa who helped design the instruments that found them. This discovery was a major contribution to science, for the radiation belts are made up of billions of mysterious particles of energy that could prove dangerous to human beings traveling through them. By finding out where these belts are and measuring their strength, Explorer I may have saved some future astronaut from death or serious injury.

Explorer I also served another useful purpose. Instead of waiting for another "scientific" rocket to send it up, space authorities agreed to launch the satellite with a standard U.S. Army Jupiter rocket. They had decided it would be foolish to waste more time trying to build and perfect new rockets when they already had military rockets that could do the job. The way was now open to use the most powerful booster in the U.S. arsenal, the Atlas rocket, as soon as it was ready, to send up larger pay loads—perhaps even a man.

It was not always a sure thing that a man would be allowed to go. Some American scientists claimed that it would be more sensible to launch only instruments into space, and to let the instruments make measurements and take photographs automatically. The main reason for this argument was that the instruments would be expendable and could be abandoned, if necessary, whereas a man could not. And the instruments could also be sent up sooner and with far less effort than it would take to send up the heavy equipment necessary to keep a man alive in space and bring him back.

This argument made a certain amount of sense. Space was—and is— a hostile environment that no one knows very much about. It is saturated with billions of tiny meteorites, any one of which could penetrate a space capsule or even an astronaut's space suit and cause a tragic failure. A man

The American answer to the Sputniks was the Navy's Vanguard rocket, scheduled to orbit a test satel

December 6, 1957. But after rising a few feet, the Vanguard blew up—as seen in this eyewitness painting.

in space would also be at the mercy of sudden solar flares of high energy radiation. The exposure of an astronaut inside a sealed capsule to radiation of this intensity could cause radiation sickness similar to that suffered by atomic bomb victims, as Explorer I had discovered.

Besides these problems, some scientists also argued that sending up a man was nothing more than a grandstand stunt that would be more expensive to pull off than it was worth. Men could accomplish nothing in space, these particular scientists repeated, that the instruments could not do better.

But there was a strong answer for that argument. The astronomers and

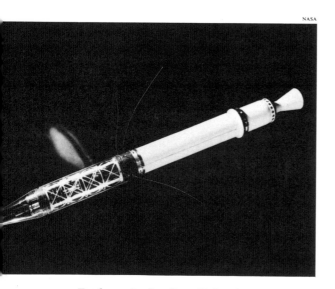

NASA

Explorer I, the first U.S. object in space, was an impressive package, though only 80 inches long. At the front were four antennas to transmit space data from many instruments; the motor of the rocket is at the rear.

weather men had always claimed it would be ideal if some of them could go up into space along with their instruments. They wanted to study conditions with their own eyes and be able to make last-minute adjustments of the instruments in case conditions changed during a flight. Also, some of the space engineers thought it would be best to send trained pilots along to monitor the complex equipment in the spacecraft itself and to take over the controls if anything went wrong.

As the hour of decision neared, there was agreement on only two points: it would be less trouble to send up a machine; and once up, a machine could survive longer in space than a man. As one Air Force general put it, "Man is the only element in the entire [space capsule] system that you can't just plug in and out like a radio tube. But," the general added, "man *can* do things that an instrument cannot. He can think better than a robot. He can rely on his human intelligence and courage to figure a way out of emergencies, which a machine cannot. And he is a trained observer who can come back to earth and tell us exactly how it *feels* out there, or how the cabin actually *smelled* when it heated up, or exactly what *shade* of color there was where the atmosphere ended. We want to know all those things, too."

This kind of reasoning won the day, and the engineers were told to go ahead. They decided to be extremely cautious and to take each step slowly

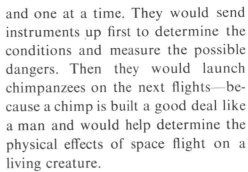

and one at a time. They would send instruments up first to determine the conditions and measure the possible dangers. Then they would launch chimpanzees on the next flights—because a chimp is built a good deal like a man and would help determine the physical effects of space flight on a living creature.

And then, when the engineers were satisfied that their techniques were reasonably foolproof, they would start launching men. The first men would go up on short flights to test the system once more and to reconnoiter this dangerous new frontier of space. The later flights with men would become progressively longer and longer until everyone was satisfied the system was sound.

Although the engineers would proceed with a great deal of caution in an effort to avoid failures, they also knew they had no time to waste. The Russians were already making such great strides that the United States would have to move at a steady pace if it was ever going to catch up.

The engineers decided that the best way to streamline the program was to get started on everything at once. That is, while one group of engineers concentrated on getting the instruments

Boosting Explorer I into space was a Jupiter-C rocket, developed from German V-2s and Army Redstones. The satellite rode on top of the rocket's third stage, a rotating cluster of rockets that resembled a tub.

ready that would go up first, other experts would start preparing the chimpanzee flights that would go next, and still other teams would start training the men who would go last. In this way, there would be no delay, and the U.S. space program would be able to move right along from one step to the next.

It had taken years for the United States to make the big decision to explore space. But once the decision was made, the work began in earnest. The National Aeronautics and Space Administration (NASA), the government agency which was set up to manage the tremendous program, was officially opened for business on October 1, 1958. Just five days later, NASA's first administrator, Dr. T. Keith Glennan, was given a detailed briefing on plans to send a manned satellite into space. Dr. Glennan's decision was quick and firm. "Let's get on with it," he said.

Project Mercury, as the first program was called, was given the highest government priority so that it could procure the money, the special equipment, and the skilled manpower that NASA needed. Within three weeks after Dr. Glennan made his decision, the first designs for building a manned spacecraft were submitted to U.S. industry to see which firms were interested in the program and capable of handling the difficult job.

Four months later, in February, 1959, a government contract to build the spacecraft was awarded to the McDonnell Aircraft Corporation of St. Louis, Missouri. McDonnell had had experience in helping to develop and produce airplanes for the U.S. Navy, and its engineers and technicians went right to work turning out models of the Mercury spacecraft in order to test the design.

In the meantime, while this work was going on, NASA began its search for a team of pilots who would be trained as the nation's first astronauts. The requirements that NASA laid down were stiff and very specific. NASA already knew that the Mercury spacecraft would be only seventy inches wide at the bottom (so it could fit exactly on top of the Redstone and Atlas rockets that were already being built). NASA engineers figured that no astronaut could fit inside this capsule—especially when he had his bulky boots, spacesuit, and helmet on—if he was any taller than 5'11". This decision ruled out a lot of well-qualified men who were six feet tall or over, but it had to be.

The age limit for the astronauts was set at 40, on the theory that any astronaut who was older than that would probably be too old for space flight by the time the rockets were ready to take him. The weight limit was set at 180 pounds. The men would have to be in perfect physical shape, of course, and the doctors felt that men who weighed more than 180 might have trouble adjusting their systems to the rigors of space flight.

Because NASA was looking for men who could react with coolness

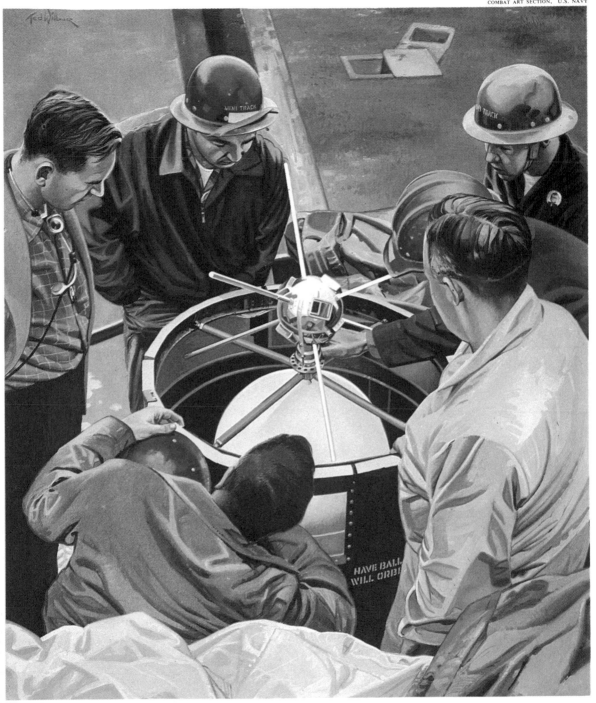

Here the Vanguard satellite is fitted to its rocket harness. But was there room for a manned vehicle?

and quick precision to any mechanical emergencies that might crop up, it limited its search to experienced jet test pilots who had already demonstrated their ability to perform well under hazardous conditions. NASA also laid down the stipulation that the men would be expected to pitch in from the start with engineering advice in order to help the program get going. Because of this, they were required to have the equivalent of a college degree in aeronautical engineering.

Finding young men who met all of these requirements was a big order. NASA started by searching the rosters of U.S. test pilots and came up with a master list of 508 possible candidates who seemed to fit the major requirements. This list, which was much too long, was quickly whittled down to 110 men with the help of questionnaires and advice from senior test pilots who knew the men well.

Another screening brought the list to 69 men, who were then given ex-tensive personal interviews by NASA representatives to determine how many of them were actually interested in volunteering for the project. A total of 37 men dropped out at this point, leaving 32 candidates who then had to go through a strenuous series of physical and mental examinations to pick out the strongest. A total of 18 men survived these tests. And from this group NASA picked the men it wanted.

After looking over the schedule of work that had to be done in the months and years ahead, NASA decided that at the start it would need a group of seven astronauts to carry out the mission of Project Mercury. So seven were chosen, and on April 9, 1959, the first American pioneers for space were introduced to the public at a press conference in Washington. They were (from right to left below):

SCOTT CARPENTER, age 34, weight 160, height 5'10", light brown hair,

Life MAGAZINE (c) 1959 TIME

Seven smiling and eager astronauts met the press in April, 1959.

green eyes. A U.S. Navy test pilot from Boulder, Colorado, Carpenter liked to swim, jump on a trampoline, and play the guitar for relaxation.

GORDON COOPER, the youngest of the group at 32, weight 150, height 5'9-1/2", brown hair, blue eyes. An Air Force test pilot from Shawnee, Oklahoma, Cooper liked to fly his own plane for relaxation, was also fond of photography, water-skiing, hunting, and fishing.

JOHN GLENN, the oldest at 38, weight 180, height 5'10", red hair, green eyes. A Marine Corps test pilot who had flown combat missions in the Pacific in World War II and had shot down three Communist MIGs over Korea. Glenn was born in Cambridge, Ohio, and liked to water-ski in his spare time.

VIRGIL GRISSOM (better known as Gus), age 33, weight 155, the shortest astronaut at 5'7", brown hair and eyes. An Air Force test pilot from Mitchell, Indiana, with a degree in mechanical engineering from Purdue University, Grissom had flown 100 combat missions over Korea, liked to hunt and fish.

WALTER SCHIRRA, age 36, weight 185 (he had to slim down to make the team), height 5'10", brown hair and eyes. A Navy test pilot from Hackensack, New Jersey, Schirra was a graduate of the U.S. Naval Academy at Annapolis and had fought in Korea. He was fond of sports cars and waterskiing.

ALAN SHEPARD, age 35, weight 160, the tallest astronaut at 5'11", brown hair and blue eyes. Born in Derry, New Hampshire, he was also a graduate of the U.S. Naval Academy. Shepard was an experienced Navy test pilot who had helped perfect several Navy jet fighters. He was the leading golfer on the team.

DONALD SLAYTON (better known as Deke), age 35, weight 160, height 5'10-1/2", brown hair and blue eyes. An Air Force test pilot from Sparta, Wisconsin, he flew combat missions over both Europe and Japan in World War II. Slayton completed four years of college in two years (including an aeronautical engineering degree) by doubling up on his classes. He was especially fond of fishing.

When the astronauts had their first press conference, a reporter asked any one of them who felt that he was ready to go into space right away to hold up his hand. This was rather a premature question, for there were still years of frustrating work ahead. But the astronauts were game—and they were confident. All seven men raised their right hands. Two of them —John Glenn and Wally Schirra— laughingly raised both hands. The team was raring to go.

4

TRAINING THE SEVEN

The seven men had much in common. They were all dedicated, experienced pilots. They were all married and had children. They were all so highly motivated and anxious to go into space that each of the seven wanted in the worst way to be the first. But the men were also different from each other in many ways.

"There's no doubt about it," one of them explained one day. "We are seven different individuals. We all have different abilities and temperaments. But I think we balance each other out pretty well."

This mixture of personality and skills was exactly what NASA wanted and needed. There was so much work to do and so little time in which to do it that each of the astronauts was expected to pitch in and share all that he knew or could learn with all of the other men on the team. Scott Car-

penter, for example, had had intensive training in the Navy in communications and navigation. So he buckled down to specialize on these subjects as they pertained to space flight, and he shared what he learned with the other six.

John Glenn had had experience helping to design airplane cockpits, so he took on the job of supervising the location of all the hundreds of switches, dials, meters, and control handles that would have to be crammed inside the spacecraft. Glenn knew that the force of gravity would be pulling against the astronauts during their flights and that they would not be able to move their heads or hands back and forth very easily to look at the controls or to reach for them. So he saw to it that all the instruments were placed where the astronauts could find them quickly.

Because Walter Schirra had been in the Navy and was familiar with the Navy pressure suit that was being adapted to provide space suits for the astronauts, he took on the responsibility for checking this item. Gus Grissom had studied a good deal of

Gathered around an experimental model of a spacecraft, the seven Americans chosen for Project Mercury are (from the right, clockwise) astronauts Cooper, Carpenter, Shepard, Grissom, Slayton, Glenn, and Schirra.

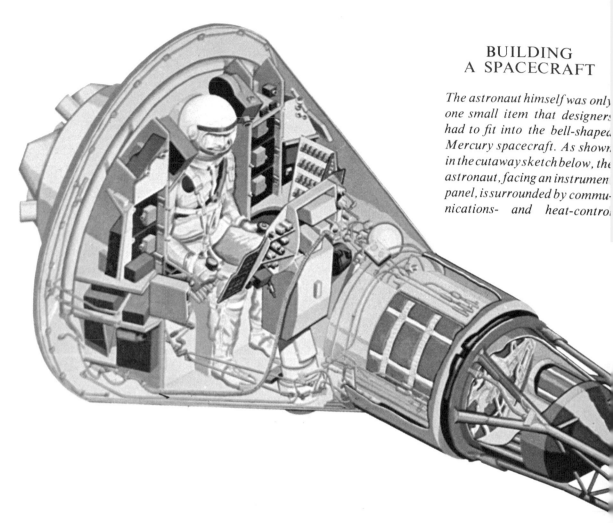

*The astronaut himself was only
one small item that designers
had to fit into the bell-shaped
Mercury spacecraft. As shown
in the cutaway sketch below, the
astronaut, facing an instrument
panel, is surrounded by commu-
nications- and heat-control*

technical engineering, so he concentrated on the complicated control systems that would keep the spacecraft
in the proper position during a flight.

Gordon Cooper headed out to the
Army Redstone Arsenal in Huntsville,
Alabama, where Dr. von Braun and
his associates were preparing the Redstone missiles that would launch the
astronauts on their first short training
flights. Deke Slayton concentrated on
the Atlas rocket that was still being
perfected and helped make sure that
it was as safe and dependable as possi-

ble before the men would be allowed
to ride on top of it.

And Alan Shepard, who had had
considerable experience with the top
command of the U.S. Navy, went to
work helping plan the intricate system
of tracking and communications stations that would circle the earth in a
continuous chain to keep track of the
astronauts during their long orbital
flights. Shepard also helped to devise
the rescue techniques that the Navy
would use to fish the astronauts out of
the water after a landing.

gear. In the craft's forward compartment and nose are parachutes to ease it back to earth; attached to the nose is an escape tower that ends in a solid-fuel rocket motor to pull the spacecraft clear of the booster in case of trouble. The painting at right shows the capsule and tower being put into place atop a rocket before lift-off.

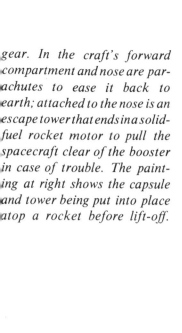

The engineers knew it was possible that an orbiting astronaut might run into trouble and have to come down on dry land somewhere; and they made provisions for this in their emergency plans and training. But since most of the orbital path would be over water—especially in the areas off Florida where all of the flights would begin and many of them would end— the engineers concentrated on finding ways to use the ocean as a landing platform.

Once all of this work was farmed out, the biggest job was to coordinate it so that everything came out even

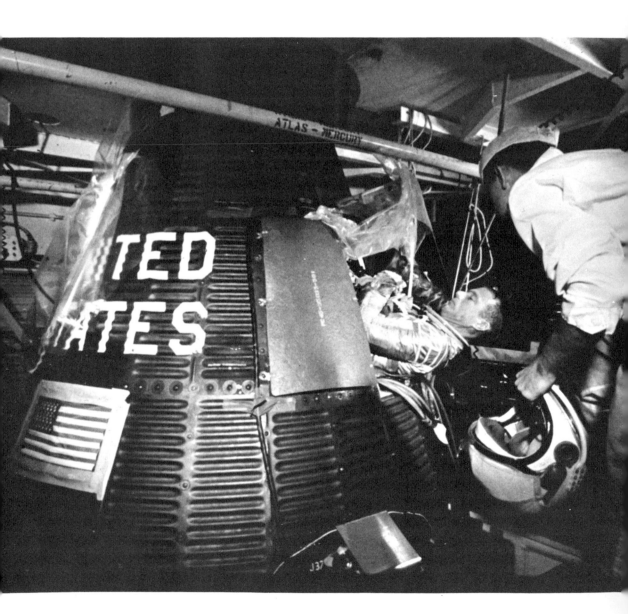

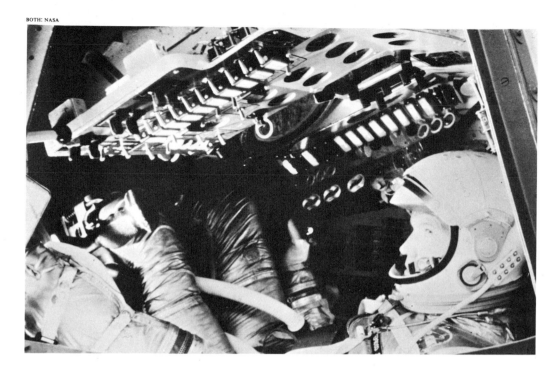

TESTING THE CAPSULE FOR SIZE

The capsule's final design was set only after it had been thoroughly tested by the astronauts. They could just squeeze into the main hatch—Scott Carpenter shows how in the photograph opposite. Once inside the 6 by 9 foot interior, there was barely enough room to perform flight functions. Above, Gordon Cooper works controls that activate steering jets in the fuselage.

and nothing fell too far behind. On some weeks the astronauts studied together at their first headquarters at Langley Air Force Base in Virginia. At other times they split up and traveled around the country to various space installations and then met again at Langley to compare notes and trade information.

One of the most difficult problems the astronauts and NASA engineers faced was to make sure that the spacecraft and the rockets that would lift it into space fitted together perfectly.

If the two components did not fit together, they might damage each other during take-off and endanger a mission. This problem was made more complicated by the fact that each component was being built by a different manufacturer at separate plants hundreds of miles apart. And each component was a completely different kind of machine that had never been used in this way before.

The Atlas, for example, was a rocket about 80 feet tall that was originally designed to propel a nuclear war head,

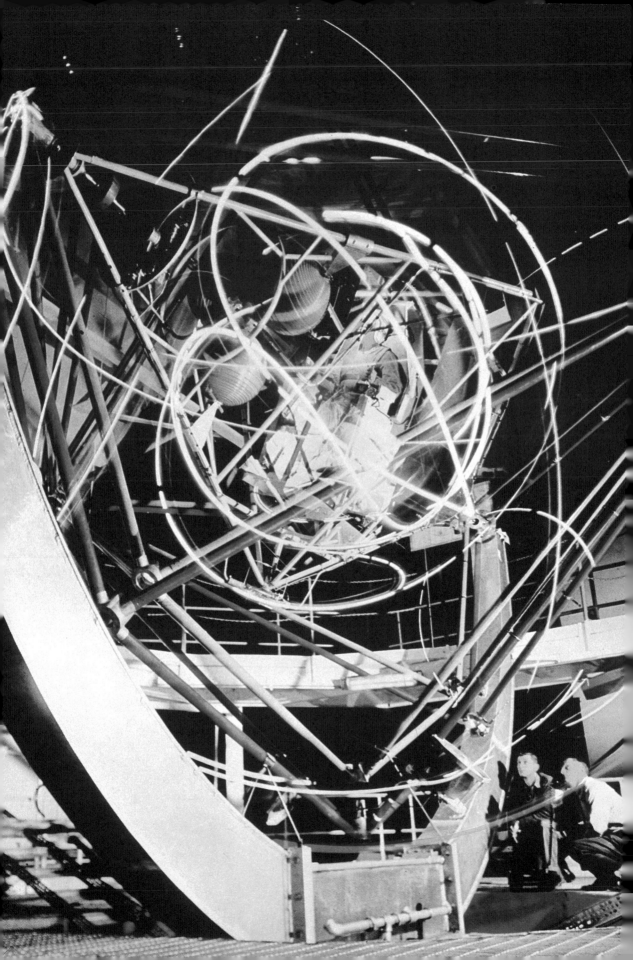

not a man. It was put together with such a complicated maze of wiring, pipes, pumps, bolts, controls, and connections that a tiny error in any one part might cause a malfunction that could blow the whole thing up at any moment during a launching. (To help avoid this, the Atlas was equipped with a special electronic warning system that kept track of all the working parts during a manned flight and could automatically separate the spacecraft from the Atlas in a split second in case of danger.)

The Atlas was quite an improvement over Dr. Goddard's early rockets. It had three big engines instead of just one—a powerful main engine in the tail that was called the sustainer, and two smaller engines fastened to the outside of the cylinder that were called boosters. The two boosters were designed to help the Atlas build up extra speed during lift-off. After two minutes of flight they dropped away automatically in order to lighten the load. The sustainer engine went on working until just before the spacecraft went into orbit.

Altogether, the three engines could build up more than 360,000 pounds of thrust. This tremendous power tended to make the Atlas shimmy and shake quite a bit as it went up. One of Deke Slayton's worries was to make sure this problem was ironed out as much as possible so that the vibrating Atlas would not damage the spacecraft on top of it or endanger the astronaut inside.

It was also possible that the spacecraft could damage the Atlas. For when the capsule was fully loaded with the pilot and all of the equipment and supplies he needed for a flight, it weighed about two tons. This was a

SIMULATING SPACE FLIGHT

Other tests and training trials the astronauts endured included simulated flights in space. Just as a capsule might spin wildly when in space, the whirling chair in the photograph opposite is spun on three different axes simultaneously by test engineers; the man in the chair tries to counter these motions with his hand controls. At right, astronauts experience a brief, though not unpleasant, period of weightlessness inside a plane.

"SUITING UP"

In his silvery space suit, Gordon Cooper (right) looks something like an armored knight. He is indeed armored—against the perils of space—with both new devices and material that had been designed for earlier flights. The most important feature of the suit is that it is pressure inflatable (an air hose plugs into the socket on the left side) to protect the astronaut against a possible puncture in the hull. Thus, air flows between the suit and the astronaut's "long johns," which are visible in the picture of John Glenn dressing opposite. A technician assisting Glenn holds a folded-up suit and has set out special equipment: the chest mirror, to reflect the instruments for better camera advantage, and wrist mirrors, to help the astronaut see anywhere inside the craft.

it was shaped more like the lid of a garbage pail.

There was a sound engineering reason for this. The blunt end was the section that would be pointed toward earth as the spacecraft re-entered the atmosphere after a flight. The engineers knew the spacecraft should not come back *too* fast. If it did, the spacecraft would simply build up extra friction against the atmosphere and get so hot it might burn up. Because the astronaut would be lying on his couch just inside the blunt end of the capsule, the engineers had to be extremely careful to keep this end as cool as possible.

To accomplish this important feat, the bottom end of the spacecraft was equipped with a heatshield, a thick layer of special material that would start to vaporize, or boil off, as the temperature increased. As the heatshield material flashed into vapor, it would carry off some of the excess heat with it, and this would help keep the bottom end cool and prevent the astronaut from roasting to death inside.

The astronaut would lie in a prone position across the bottom of the capsule. The engineers decided on this because medical tests had shown that this position would help him absorb the tremendous force of gravity that he would experience during the flight —especially when the rocket was blasting him away from earth at a high speed. Gravity would work against the astronaut in much the

heavier load than the thin metal skin of the Atlas was originally designed to support. So the casing of the Atlas had to be reinforced—without making it too heavy—to prevent it from crumpling under the weight of its new pay load.

To make it as easy as possible for the Atlas, the engineers trimmed every pound out of the spacecraft that they could. Even so, it was a bulky-looking object. It looked more like a giant TV tube than anything else. And though the sides of the spacecraft were sloped inward to give it some streamlining on the ride up, the blunt bottom end of

77

TRACKING
THE FLIGHT

A vital part of early Mercury planning was the setting up of a tracking system. At right, a ship with special radar gear steams to her tracking station in the mid-Atlantic. From there, as from seventeen other stations all over the world, observations would be sent to the Goddard Space Flight Center in Maryland. In the Mercury Control Center at Cape Kennedy (below), information received from the capsule itself would be monitored by specialists at control consoles, and plotted on a wall-sized world map.

BOTH:

same way that it makes a person feel heavy and tend to lean over sideways when a car he is riding in speeds around a curve. In this case, the centrifugal force set up by the speed of the car on the curve tends to cancel out the force of gravity that pulls straight down on the passenger, and he is tugged off to one side.

The astronaut, however, is being shot straight up—directly away from the downward pull of gravity—and the grip of gravity works so hard to restrain him that he is pushed back into his specially designed couch with tremendous force. Depending on how fast the astronaut is moving away from earth, gravity could pull at him so hard that he would actually weigh several times his normal weight. But by lying more or less flat in the couch with only his knees raised slightly, the astronaut's body could distribute this extra weight and overcome it without serious damage.

There was also the problem of supplying air equipment and breathing oxygen—not only for the astronaut's sealed spacesuit, but also for the cabin itself. The atmosphere inside the cabin would keep the astronaut comfortable and safe in case something suddenly went wrong with the suit. This was an example of what the engineers called the back-up principle. That is, every system inside the spacecraft, from radios to controls, was reinforced, or backed up, by a second, or stand-by, system that would take over automatically in case something happened

to the first one. The engineers worked out alternates for every system—and sometimes thought up more than one alternate just to make sure.

To help the engineers down on the ground keep fully informed about how all these systems were working during a flight—and how the astronaut himself was getting along—the designers put still another system into the capsule that would send down a constant stream of information about each separate activity. This special communication system was called telemetry, and it accomplished its job by converting each fact about the capsule into a tiny blip of radio energy that was then transmitted down to the ground. When it reached the control, or tracking, station down below, the blip was translated back into a number that the engineers could read on their big display boards. In this way they could know the complete status of the astronaut and the spacecraft.

The facts that were sent down by telemetry included the astronaut's own temperature and his heartbeat; the temperature inside the spacecraft and the suit; the amount of oxygen left in the supply for the astronaut to breathe; and how much fuel was left to run the controls. All these vital facts were transmitted automatically. Even if the astronaut was incapacitated or too busy to worry about them, the data would keep flowing to the engineers on the ground, who could spot any trouble immediately. If the trouble

79

involved the astronaut himself and indicated that he was unable to function, the engineers could radio instructions up to the spacecraft and it could start bringing itself back to earth.

This was one of the trickiest features of the Mercury spacecraft (although it was designed to be flown eventually by a pilot). But since the first flights had no passengers at all, and the next ones had only chimpanzees on board, obviously the spacecraft had to be able to fly automatically. The automatic controls were left in during the astronaut flights to act as a back-up for the pilots in case something happened to them. As it turned out, however, the human astronauts proved to be more dependable than some of the machinery. On some flights, when the automatic pilot was scheduled to perform a maneuver but failed to work, the astronauts acted as a back-up for *it* and managed to bring the spacecraft home all by themselves.

The most important function that both the astronaut and his automatic pilot had to perform was to keep the spacecraft aligned at the proper angle, or "attitude," during flight. It was not possible to make the spacecraft change its course. Once the rocket tossed the spacecraft into orbit, the capsule was headed along a predetermined path with so much speed and momentum that it stayed on that same path until it was time to slow down and come home. But the astronaut could alter the attitude of his spacecraft along this path. He could make it face forward or backward, for example, or tilt it up or down for a better view out the window.

All this was done by means of tiny rocket motors mounted on the outside of the spacecraft and fueled with hydrogen peroxide that could exhaust superheated steam and make the spacecraft change its position. There were three different directions the spacecraft could move in, and all three were handled by a single control stick. The capsule could be made to "yaw," or twist, from side to side the way a crab crawls along a beach. It could "pitch"—point itself downward toward the earth or up toward the stars. Or it could "roll," that is, rotate in a circle to the left or right, depending on which way the astronaut wanted to go and which tiny jets he activated to shift the capsule in that direction.

Placing his right hand on the control stick, the astronaut could control yaw by twisting the stick in his hand like a water faucet. If he wanted to roll to the left or right, he simply moved the stick sideways in the appropriate direction. And he pulled straight back on the stick or pushed it straight forward to make the capsule pitch up or down.

The astronauts knew that they would need a lot of practice to perfect this technique because it was completely new. Pilots normally use a stick to control the pitch or roll of an airplane, but they use their feet on a

SURVIVING ANYWHERE ON EARTH

The astronauts had to be ready to cope with conditions anywhere on earth in case their capsules did not land in the mid-ocean recovery zones. Because the projected orbital paths passed over deserts in Australia and Africa, desert survival was given special attention. In the picture below, the seven astronauts, wearing protective outfits made from parachutes, are shown how to construct a shelter. At left, Scott Carpenter attempts to make a chain from his parachute shrouds.

81

ESCAPING AT SEA

If his flight ended as planned, an astronaut would have to climb out of a half-submerged capsule into the open sea. Simulating that maneuver, Virgil Grissom, opposite, squeezes out the narrow neck of a training capsule; at right, Scott Carpenter tests an inflatable life raft and other sea-survival gear.

rudder to make it yaw. The astronauts had to learn to fly all over again and combine all these maneuvers in one complicated handle.

This was not the only novelty they had to get used to. Everything about space flight was new and different. And since there is no real way to practice actual space flight without going on a mission, they had to do the next best thing—rehearse each maneuver on training devices that at least gave them the general idea.

One of these devices was called the centrifuge. John Glenn called this "the most spectacular and most valuable of all the training machines we got to climb into." Located at a Navy laboratory in Johnsville, Pennsylvania, the centrifuge consisted of a huge steel arm 50 feet long that could spin around at tremendous speeds. The long arm had an enclosed cockpit attached to one end of it. The astronaut rode inside the cockpit with a replica of the spacecraft instrument

panel and controls in front of him.

As he whirled faster and faster (the arm could spin at speeds up to 48 revolutions per second) the force of gravity would weigh so heavily on the astronaut that his face would be distorted out of shape, and his eyeballs would feel as though they were coming loose. The astronauts often became very dizzy on these rides, and sometimes they had trouble breathing under the tremendous pressure. But they soon learned to conquer these sensations and to keep working at the controls under conditions far more difficult than anything they would actually feel in space. It was excellent practice.

While all this was going on, the spacecraft was also being put through a strenuous physical workout. Just to make sure that it could stand up under all the maximum conditions it might run into, the capsule was submitted by the engineers to all kinds of mechanized torture. It was slammed into water to make sure it would hold up and float after a bumpy landing. It was banged into sand to see what might happen if it came down off course and landed in a desert. It was even dropped onto solid concrete as a final test of its ability to withstand shock. In addition to these drop tests, the engineers placed models of the spacecraft in a jet flame at 6,000 degrees to prove that it would survive the tremendous heat of re-entry.

All of this work took more than two years on the part of the engineers, the manufacturers, and the astronauts themselves. Project Mercury was so complicated that quite often something went wrong with one phase of it that delayed progress in other areas. And some Americans, who felt frustrated that the United States was taking so long to get a man into space, criticized NASA for being too cautious. NASA's answer was the same each time. "Our purpose is not to take chances and cut corners looking for a quick success," the engineers said. "Our job is to send American pilots into space *and* get them back safely."

The engineers were rewarded. In due time most of the major problems were solved and things came out fairly even. It was time now for the pay-off. Commander Shepard was chosen to be the first American to go into space. His mission would be a short, ballistic flight—like a bullet fired into the air and curving right back down again. The purpose of this flight was to give a man his first ride into space inside

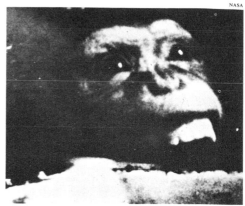

These frames from a film taken on board a Mercury spacecraft show Ham, the chimp sent up before Shepard. He grimaces in reaction to the pressures of a flight that was longer, higher, and faster than expected.

the Mercury capsule and see if the systems and the controls responded in the manner that a trained pilot wanted them to.

Before Shepard was allowed to go, however, NASA stuck to its original plan and sent a 37-pound chimpanzee up first to see what effect the ride would have on him. The chimp's name

84

was Ham, and he had a fairly rough time. Wires were fastened to Ham in several places so instruments could send back a flow of data on Ham's responses by telemetry. All of this worked fine.

However, a few things did go wrong with the spacecraft and with the Redstone rocket that sent Ham up. For one thing, the Redstone produced more power and speed than the engineers had figured on, and it went higher into space and about 130 miles farther down range than they wanted it to. This meant that Ham overshot the recovery ships that had been cruising around in a predetermined target area waiting for him. And by the time the nearest ship could reach the spacecraft, the capsule had sprung a leak and was taking on water. Fortunately, Ham was snug and dry inside a sealed compartment. But he was angry and upset at the rough ride he had had, and the next time his trainers showed Ham a spacecraft, the chimp bared his teeth and refused to go anywhere near it.

Despite this reaction, Ham—who made his flight on the last day of January, 1961—came out of it in good physical shape. He proved that a living creature could take the Mercury ride without ill effects. Just a few weeks later, on April 12, the Soviet Union stole the headlines once more by announcing that one of its cosmonauts, Major Yuri Gagarin, had orbited the earth once in a Sputnik in 108 minutes. This was a tremendous jump over

what the United States was prepared to do. But NASA went on with its plans. For before the United States could put a man into orbit, it had to make sure that its own system of space flight was practical and sound. It was Alan Shepard's job to prove that, and Shepard was ready.

In April, 1961, three months after Ham's flight, the Soviet Union put the first man in orbit. Having completed one full circuit, Major Yuri Gagarin landed safely on a collective farm—to receive the adulation of an admiring world and gain a chestful of medals.

5

FIRST UP

All of the astronauts spent a lot of time trying to get the nation used to the idea that, despite their reputations, they were not really supermen at all, just normal, red-blooded Americans. There were no great differences between them and the average American, they tried to claim—except, perhaps, for some unusual experience as jet test pilots, a better than average physique, and a willingness to attempt something that would have frightened most people to death. Flying was so much in their blood, the astronauts maintained, that what they were about to do was nothing more than an extension of what they had been doing all along.

There was one man who knew the astronauts almost as well as most of them knew themselves, and who did not always agree with this theory. He was Air Force Lieutenant Colonel William K. Douglas, a friendly, soft-spoken medical officer who served as the astronauts' personal physician from the time they joined the program and looked out after them until it was time for their launchings. "The morning each man went into space," Bill Douglas said, "was the only time when he was *not* normal, when he *was* a superman . . ."

Douglas should know. It was he who woke up Alan Shepard on the morning of May 5, 1961. The doctor said that when he went in and woke up the astronaut, he "acted just as if he were going out duck hunting or starting on a fishing trip." Shepard himself admitted later that he had some "butterflies" in his stomach—in other words, he was normally nervous. And he had good reason to be. For Shepard was the first American ever to sit on top of a high-powered rocket and ride it into space. His mission would last only 15 minutes and 22 seconds—not nearly so long as the flight Yuri Gagarin had just made for Russia. But because the Mercury flight system had not been thoroughly tested yet—this was part of Shepard's job—

Workers look from the gantry as it is rolled back with the plastic-fronted "green-house," leaving Alan Shepard sealed in his capsule atop the Redstone rocket. He was there, 70 feet up, for five hours before the launch.

86

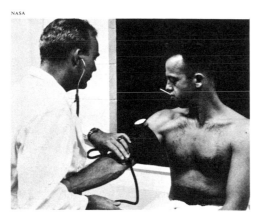

Medical officer William K. Douglas checks Shepard's blood pressure and temperature.

the event would be every bit as dangerous as it was historic.

But as far as anyone could tell just by looking at him that morning, Shepard regarded the assignment as a routine flight. It was about one o'clock A.M. when he was awakened by Bill Douglas. Then he put on a bathrobe and sat down for a hearty breakfast of orange juice, a steak wrapped in bacon, and scrambled eggs.

When he had finished eating, Shepard walked into the medical room for a final examination. Douglas and the other doctors had already satisfied themselves that the astronaut was in excellent shape. He had a loose toenail where someone had stepped on his toe, and he had a sunburn from being in Florida so long. But, other than that, he was in his usual fine physical condition.

After the examination, Shepard started "suiting up" for the mission.

This took about 20 minutes. A few wires were taped to various parts of his body to record his physical reactions later over the telemetry network. Then, with the help of Joe Schmitt, the NASA technician who dressed all of the astronauts for their flights, Shepard started squirming into his tight, rubberized space suit. The heavy boots and special gloves went on next. The gloves were zippered onto the arms of his suit so there would be no leaks for the oxygen to escape from inside the system. The suit weighed about 25 pounds and fitted very tightly, so it was not easy to move around from then on.

Meanwhile, out on the launching pad, the NASA technicians were making one final check of the Redstone rocket. It had already been loaded with its supply of fuel and liquid oxygen—roughly the same mixture that Dr. Goddard had used 30 years before. John Glenn, who had stood by as Shepard's back-up pilot until the last minute, went out to peer inside the spacecraft to make sure it was completely ready.

A little after five o'clock that morning, Shepard arrived at the launching pad in a huge air-conditioned trailer and took an elevator up to the top of the Redstone gantry where the spacecraft, bearing the name Freedom 7,

With the slow stride of a man wearing a 25-pound suit, Shepard approaches the elevator that will take him to the top of the rocket.

was waiting. It was still two hours before lift-off, but Shepard said he wanted to look things over—sort of "kick the tires" as a test pilot would call checking out a new airplane. On the way up, Bill Douglas had handed Shepard a box of crayons. This referred to an old joke about an astronaut who was taking a coloring book along with him into space to help kill time, but then refused to go at the last minute because he forgot his crayons. Shepard laughed at the joke —it helped relieve the tension—and handed the crayons back to Douglas. He said he thought he would have enough to do that day without them.

At 5:20 Shepard climbed into the spacecraft and started strapping him-self into the form-fitting couch that would help him absorb the punishing force of gravity. Technicians helped him get settled. Then Shepard closed the faceplate on his helmet. This meant that from then on he had to talk with the men around him through a radio microphone.

There were quite a few people Shepard could talk to. Gordon Cooper, one of his fellow astronauts, was stationed inside the big concrete blockhouse not far from the launching pad keeping tabs on the weather downrange where Shepard would be picked up. Deke Slayton was at a console inside the Mercury Control Center, where he would do most of the talking to Shepard during the flight.

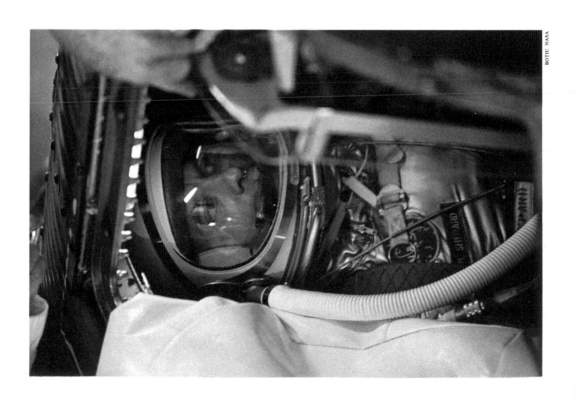

John Glenn had finished his main work by now. So had Gus Grissom, who had kept Shepard company that morning during breakfast and on the long ride out to the pad. Glenn and Grissom left the launching area and joined Slayton at the control center. Walter Schirra and Scott Carpenter waited on an Air Force field nearby, ready to take off in two fast jet fighters to chase Shepard's rocket as far out over the Atlantic Ocean as possible to keep an eye on the spacecraft until it disappeared.

The entire astronaut team was ready—including Shepard. But not everything else was. At 7:14, two hours after Alan Shepard climbed into his spacecraft, and only 15 min-

utes before the Redstone was scheduled to leave the ground, a thick layer of clouds started drifting in over the area, forcing the NASA officials inside the control center to declare a delay, or "hold." They needed perfect visibility in order to track the Redstone on its way up. So it was necessary to wait until the weather cleared.

Then another problem cropped up. During the delay for weather, a small electrical device inside the Redstone began to overheat. The device had to work perfectly in order to provide power for the Redstone's insides. So it was necessary to call for another delay while technicians replaced the device. This took 86 precious minutes.

During these delays, Alan Shepard

Strapped on his back in the capsule, Shepard watches while the hatch is closed (opposite). From the blockhouse, Gordon Cooper (above) keeps in touch with Shepard and waits for the countdown.

lay back patiently in his couch and kept calm. He knew what the troubles were by listening to the conversations over his earphones. The doctors monitored his condition and could see from watching their instruments inside the control center that he was suffering little physical strain. His blood pressure, heartbeat, and breathing rate were normal considering the circumstances (they were slightly higher than when he was *not* about to take off on a rocket). And Shepard helped himself keep cool and collected by looking through his periscope at the view outside. He could see technicians running around down below him on the pad and the ocean waves beating against the beach nearby.

There were two more short delays to give the technicians time to double-check some mechanical details. Then, at 9:34 A.M., more than five hours after he had climbed on board, Shepard heard Deke Slayton calling out the countdown for him. "Ten, nine, eight, seven, six, five, four, three, two, one, lift-off!" A red-hot flame roared out of the Redstone's tail and swept across the concrete launching pad. For a second the Redstone rocket seemed to hesitate. Then, slowly at first, it began to climb.

Just before lift-off, the ground crew folded up the yellow "cherry picker"—a derrick into which Shepard could have climbed at the last moment. Then the 33-ton rocket lifted from the pad. Freedom 7 was on its way.

Inside the control center, the men who were most responsible for Shepard's safety kept their eyes glued to a series of display boards that showed the telemetry data as it came flowing. NASA officials were all concerned for Shepard's safety, but they were also confident. Everyone knew that the emergency warning system inside the Redstone could try to bring Shepard back by parachute in case of trouble. There were also emergency buttons in the control center for activating this system, and the men who monitored them kept their fingers poised. But everything was going well. The engineers watched the telemetry data closely, and this told them the rocket and spacecraft were doing fine. The men were especially relieved to hear Shepard's own voice confirm this fact over the radio. "Roger, lift-off . . ." Shepard shouted.

"Reading you loud and clear," Shepard added quickly to assure the control center that communications were good and that the men on the ground did not have to worry about that.

"This is Freedom 7," he said confidently a second or two later as he ticked off a number of important items on the check list. "The fuel is 'Go'." (He was referring to the availability of the hydrogen peroxide fuel that he was to use later to test the spacecraft's controls.) "One-point-two G." (This meant that the pull of gravity had increased a little. Normally a man on earth is under one G.)

"Cabin at fourteen psi." (His reading showed that the air pressure inside the cabin was at the prescribed 14 pounds per square inch to help equalize the pressure outside.) "Oxygen is 'GO.'" (This meant that both Shepard's personal supply of oxygen and the supply for the cabin were functioning perfectly.)

Shepard remarked after the flight that he probably braced himself a little more than necessary during the final countdown. He did this, he explained, because no one knew exactly how much shock and vibration he would feel when the rocket finally took off. He soon found out that the ride was not so rough as he had expected, and he was able to relax. "I knew I was going up," he said, "but the sensation was very gentle."

Immediately after lift-off and during much of the flight, Shepard kept busy communicating with the control center. Since he was the first American to fly into space, the engineers on the ground were especially anxious to hear about every detail as it happened. "We wanted to get our money's worth from this flight," said one of them, "so Al kept himself busy telling us everything and testing everything we could think of."

Two minutes and 22 seconds after he had left the ground, Shepard could feel the Redstone engine shut down right on schedule. This meant that the powered phase of the flight was over. A whole sequence of automatic events began to take place now, and Shepard described each one to Deke Slayton so the men in the control center could keep track of them too. First, the emergency escape tower that was fastened on top of the spacecraft to pull it free of the rocket in case of trouble fell away. (See sequence on page 96.)

Right after this event, Shepard could hear the firing of small rockets underneath him that forced the spacecraft and the Redstone to separate and left the spacecraft hurtling through space on its own. This was a key moment in the flight, and the telemetry readings told the doctors down below that Shepard's pulse—which normally stood at 65—had jumped temporarily to 138. The reaction was understandable. Shepard was now weightless. He had broken through the grip of gravity, and his spacecraft was now soaring through the vacuum of space on its own momentum. It would continue rising to an altitude of 116.5 miles. Then, as the spacecraft slowed down, gravity would take over again and start pulling it back to earth faster and faster until maximum velocity was reached. The heatshield would heat up at this point but would prevent the capsule from burning up in the atmosphere. Then, eventually, the huge recovery parachutes would open up to slow the descent. Finally—if everything went according to schedule—the spacecraft would splash into the ocean not far from where an aircraft carrier and other recovery ships were standing by to pick Shepard up.

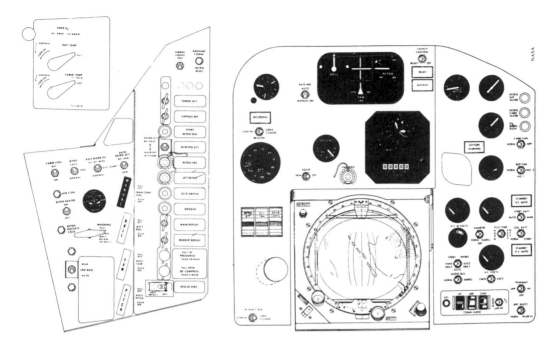

When testing the jets that controlled the spacecraft's angle of flight, Shepard checked the pitch, roll, or yaw by the alignment of pointers at the top of his instrument panel (above). As each step of the flight was completed, a light flashed on the panel (top to bottom at left). The periscope screen is at the center.

Before all this happened, however, Shepard still had a lot more work to do. Running down the check list of things NASA wanted to learn, he switched off the automatic controls that had been in operation and began to put the capsule through its paces with the manual control stick that he held in his right hand. He tried all of the maneuvers—yaw, pitch, and roll. The controls worked perfectly.

When this experiment was out of the way, Shepard turned to the next item on his schedule. He was now supposed to take a look at the view outside and determine how much visibil-ity there was from such a high altitude. (There was no picture window in Shepard's spacecraft. The engineers had left it out of their original plans. The astronauts requested a window the first chance they had—and they got one in later models. Shepard did have a periscope, however, so he peered through this at earth.)

Alan Shepard is not the kind of man who normally gets excited and makes colorful statements. But when he looked down from 100 miles up, the view beneath him was so spectacular that he could not resist saying so.

"What a beautiful sight!" Shep-

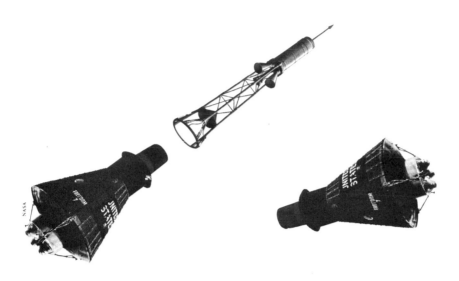

ard exclaimed into his microphone.

Looking straight down, Shepard could see the area he had just left—Cape Kennedy. Much of the United States was covered by clouds, but he could look up and down the Atlantic coast as far north as the Carolinas and as far south as the Florida Keys. Shepard also took a good look at the ocean and spotted the sharp variations in color between the deep blue of the ocean and the light green of the reefs in the Bahama Islands. "The colors were stunning," he said.

But Shepard was not looking down at the scenery just to admire it. He soon discovered that the view of earth through the periscope was so clear that sight-seeing on future flights could also be useful. The astronauts would be able to utilize the scenery to help navigate and keep track of where they were if the instruments failed.

Alan Shepard also made some mental notes on how it felt to be completely weightless for several minutes

About two minutes after lift-off, Freedom 7's Redstone rocket stops delivering thrust. Soon after, the escape tower and the rocket separate from the capsule (first phase of simulated trajectory above), which turns its blunt end forward (second phase). For five minutes, at this peak of his arc, Shepard is weightless. Then he plunges to earth (third phase), the parachute breaks out of its hold (opposite), and the craft lands 302 miles from Cape Kennedy (diagram below).

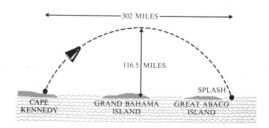

most perfectly from the moment of lift-off to the splashdown in the Atlantic, some 302 miles downrange. It proved to the engineers that the Project Mercury flight system was sound. And Alan Shepard, who had just completed the most grueling ride that any American had ever taken, brought back living proof that the American astronauts could take it and were on their way to bigger and longer adventures.

On July 21, 1961—some ten weeks after Shepard's flight—it was Gus Grissom's turn to make the second Mercury flight on a Redstone rocket. In many ways, Grissom's mission was almost identical with Shepard's. But there were a few differences. Because of a slight variation in the performance of the Redstone, Grissom's spacecraft flew about a mile and a half higher into space than Shepard's had, and it landed about a mile farther downrange. Because of this slight difference, Grissom's total flight time from launch to splashdown was 15 seconds longer than Shepard's.

But this was really of no consequence. The major difference between the two flights came at the end of Grissom's mission. His spacecraft, Liberty Bell 7, landed in the ocean and keeled over in the water as Shepard's had done. But then, before the helicopters could get to Grissom and lift his spacecraft a few feet out of the water, his escape hatch suddenly flew open prematurely and sea water rushed in through the open hatch.

ALL: NASA

Astronaut Virgil Grissom's roughest moments came not during his flight but during recovery. After the hatch of his capsule blew off prematurely, he struggled in the sea as water seeped into his suit and as helicopters trying to salvage Liberty Bell 7 made angry waves (above). At last he was pulled up (below) and taken to the stand-by ship U.S.S. Randolph. At right, damp but happy, Grissom strides across the deck of the Randolph.

The flooded capsule began to sink.

Grissom himself had a close call. He quickly dove through the open hatch into the ocean so he would not sink with the capsule. Then he treaded water in his heavy suit for several minutes while the helicopters tried to rescue his craft. It was soon filled with water, however, and became too heavy—the huge helicopters finally had to give up and let the capsule sink. The rescue crew that had been standing by then fished Grissom out. He was soaking wet but not injured.

U.S. space scientists were very disappointed to lose Grissom's spacecraft, for it went down with instruments and films that they wanted to study. But they knew from their telemetry records that the flight was a success up to that point and that the spacecraft had done its job well. On the basis of this, NASA decided to cancel further Redstone missions and move on to the next step—the big orbital flights with the Atlas. The astronauts were ready now for the big pay-off.

6

THE GREATEST ADVENTURE

Because he had served as the back-up pilot for both Alan Shepard and Gus Grissom, John Glenn was well acquainted with the Mercury spacecraft and the various things that could go wrong with it. So when the announcement was made that he would make the first orbital flight into space, Glenn knew what was expected of him. It was an assignment more complex, if not more hazardous, than any other previous flight by an American.

One thing that made it more complex was that instead of zooming up and coming right back down again in a few minutes he was scheduled to circle the earth three times on a mission that would last nearly five hours. This meant testing the capability of the spacecraft more fully than ever before. It meant that Glenn might face special mechanical problems that the other astronauts had not had to cope with on their flights. It meant that he would be under physical strain for a longer period of time. Glenn would experience the odd sensation of weightlessness far more extensively than any of the other astronauts. The medical experts were anxious to find out what ill effects, if any, this would have on him before they approved longer mis-

To dramatize the teamwork that lay behind his historic flight, John Glenn named his capsule Friendship 7. Here, technicians help the astronaut squeeze into the cockpit of the spacecraft; a plastic cover protects the corrugated shingles from accidental scratches.

Despite Glenn's eagerness, his launch was repeatedly delayed by storms. Here, NASA scientists anxiously scan weather charts.

sions for astronauts in the future.

Glenn would also have a much longer time to practice with the controls and to use the communications and other equipment in the spacecraft to help discover and iron out any bugs. And because he would ride on top of an Atlas rocket that was about five times as powerful as a Redstone, he would fly not only farther but also a lot faster than any other American had before. It would be the greatest adventure yet.

John Glenn was well aware of all these challenges. As a result, he had to prepare for his mission with great care. He had to rehearse his reactions to every kind of emergency that might be expected to occur during the flight. He had to make a detailed plan for the mission that covered every minute of it. Then he had to make sure that all of the people who would be following his progress from the ground understood what he would be doing so they could check his progress along the way. He also had to be in perfect physical shape when the day came. This meant that he had to stay in strict training during all the period of uncertainty until the day when Friendship 7 actually was lifted into orbit.

For a while, it seemed as if the day would never come. The mission was scheduled first for January 27, 1962. But just 29 minutes before the scheduled take-off—at T minus 29—the flight had to be held up temporarily because of bad weather. Then, while John Glenn stayed sealed up in his capsule and everyone waited for the weather to improve, some of the liquid fuel inside the Atlas began to leak, and the flight had to be postponed altogether to repair the leak. It was almost a month later—on February 20—that Glenn rode out to Atlas Complex 14 at Cape Kennedy (all suited up and transported in an air-conditioned van just as Al Shepard and Gus Grissom had been) and took an elevator up to the top of the Atlas gantry where the spacecraft waited for him.

Then two hours before the scheduled launch time, Colonel Glenn stuck his left foot over the sill of the open hatch and started squeezing into his tiny cockpit. At this point a small microphone inside his space helmet broke off. It had to be replaced so Glenn could communicate with the ground during the flight, and this delayed the flight for a while. Then about an hour after the microphone was fixed, there was another delay when a bolt broke as the technicians started to lock the hatch into place.

At last, however, everything was ready and the big gantry was pulled back from the Atlas, leaving John Glenn alone on top of it as the countdown proceeded. Glenn reported later that he could feel the tall Atlas swaying beneath him in the breeze and could hear all kinds of strange sounds down below inside the rocket. There was the whining and crackling of pipes inside the Atlas as the level of

ALL: NASA

On his way to the van that will take him to the launching pad, Glenn emerges from the hangar where he lived for many weeks prior to the flight. Two security guards (at right) glare at the crowd of well wishers.

OVERLEAF: *From space, Glenn saw the whole Florida peninsula and the seas around it. This picture was taken on his third orbit.*

cold liquid oxygen rose in the tanks. (Liquid oxygen has to be kept at a temperature of about 297° F. below zero to keep it from evaporating.) The whole rocket seemed to shiver as the oxygen reached the metal walls of the tanks.

There were two more brief delays before the engineers reached the end of the countdown. One delay came when a valve controlling the flow of liquid oxygen into the rocket became stuck. The second delay lasted just two minutes. It gave the engineers a chance to check on an electronic computer at the tracking station on Bermuda, several hundred miles to the east.

This was the first tracking station on the range that Glenn would reach after leaving Cape Kennedy. It was crucial that the station be working perfectly, for the engineers in the Mercury Control Center needed to have a full, instant report from Bermuda to make sure that Glenn was aimed in exactly the right direction and was flying at exactly the right speed to go into orbit. If something went wrong, they would want to bring him down immediately before he got so far out over the ocean that it would be hard to find him when he landed. But the computer was working—everything was fine.

Glenn heard this over the radio and got in a few last-minute exercises to make sure he was limbered up for the long, grueling ride. Then he put his left hand on the abort handle—which

The flight of Friendship 7 really began at the point marked "insertion" on this world map. It was there that orbital height and speed were achieved. From that "X" Glenn's 5-hour orbit is traced across the world as three overlapping tracks passing into and out of those parts that lay in darkness. Dots indicate the locations of tracking stations. Glenn came out of orbit above the West Coast ("retro-fire") and landed near Hispaniola.

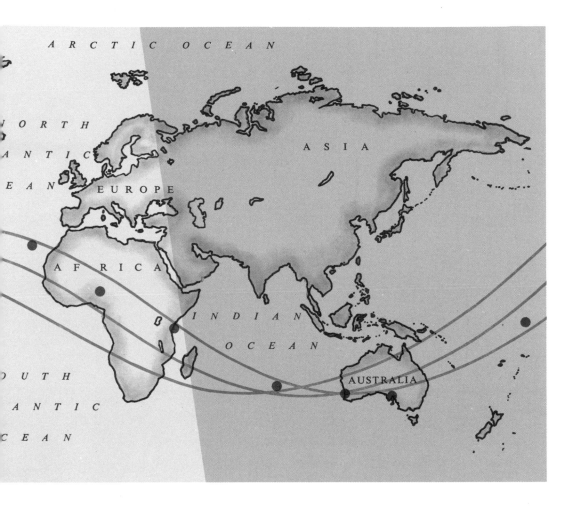

would trigger the emergency equipment to bring him back down in case he spotted trouble—and waited for the countdown. This time it came from Alan Shepard, who was performing the same chore in the control center that Deke Slayton had performed for him. (Slayton, unfortunately, was found to have a minor heart ailment, and for the moment he was dropped from further flight plans.)

At the count of zero, Glenn could hear a faint roaring sound from the engines as they started up and could feel his spacecraft begin to vibrate. Then, after a pause of a second or two while the engines built up to their correct power, the Atlas began to rise slowly off the ground, and Shepard confirmed this fact to Glenn over the radio. "The clock is operating," Glenn answered back, "we're under way."

The clock Glenn referred to was a special electric timepiece on the in-

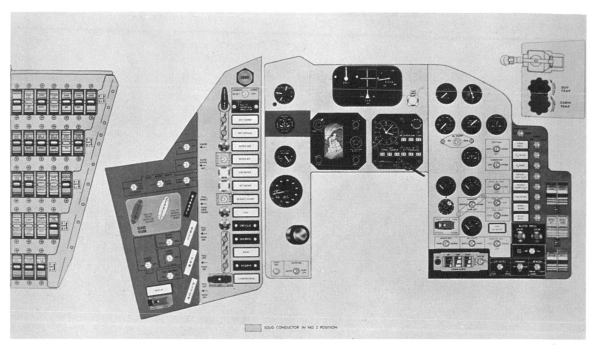

SOLID CONDUCTOR IN NO 2 POSITION

strument panel that kept track of the elapsed time during a flight. It would act like an alarm clock at the proper moment to trigger the retro-rockets that would slow the spacecraft down and start it on its way back to earth. It was crucial that the clock start operating right on time and that it stay on time throughout the flight. Since Glenn would be traveling through space at the tremendous speed of 5 miles every second, an error in the clock of only 10 seconds would mean coming down 50 miles away from the prescribed landing spot where the ships would be waiting for him. Glenn was happy to see that the clock was on time right from the start. It was a good omen.

At 2 minutes and 11 seconds after lift-off—again right on time—the two big outboard booster engines shut down and dropped away, leaving the Atlas quite a bit lighter for its final fast surge toward space. Glenn was already beyond the earth's atmosphere by this time. The air was thin here, and all the Atlas had to do now was give him a final steady push with its sustainer engine to break him completely away from the grip of gravity and toss him into orbit. Glenn re-

With raised eyebrow Glenn notes his empty tube of applesauce floating free (opposite, below). Above the periscope screen in his instrument panel (opposite, above) is a small turning globe that helps the astronaut pinpoint his location above the earth's surface.

ported that he could not feel any real sensation of speed—mostly because there were no signposts outside to look at as he whizzed along. His window was pointed up, and he could only see empty sky.

Then at precisely 5 minutes and 1.4 seconds after lift-off, the big sustainer engine shut down on schedule. A series of small explosive charges immediately pushed the spacecraft away from the Atlas and separated the two components. Now Glenn was on his own, 100 miles up, and going at the rate of 25,730 feet per second, a velocity that would free him from earth's gravity and put him into orbit. Down below in the control center, the computers quickly calculated all of this and informed Alan Shepard that conditions were perfect for a good orbital flight. Shepard immediately informed Glenn.

Now it was time for John Glenn to go to work. The flight plan called for him to orbit the earth three times, for about 90 minutes on each orbit. (Just three months before Glenn had gone up, another Atlas had put a chimpanzee, Enos, into orbit as a test. Enos was supposed to stay up for three orbits too. But the automatic controls failed, and he had to be brought down after circling the earth only twice.)

Glenn's flight plan required him to spend most of his time on the first orbit just getting used to the new environment and to the sensation of being weightless before he tried anything too tricky. Eight minutes after

From his lift-off—watched here by crowds in Grand Central Station—until his landing, Glenn was the focus of world attention.

lift-off, he was already more than halfway across the Atlantic Ocean and was testing the controls to see how they worked.

Seven minutes later he was approaching the west coast of Africa and looking out the window for his first view of the Dark Continent. Un-

fortunately, much of the earth was covered by clouds that day, but Glenn had a clear view of huge dust storms blowing across the African desert and could even see the smoke from big brush fires along the edge of the desert.

As Glenn passed over the small

island of Zanzibar, off the east coast of Africa, the NASA medical officer at the tracking station there asked Glenn how he felt. Glenn reported that he felt fine and that being weightless was no problem at all. In fact, he explained later, it was a lot of fun.

"I was busy at one moment taking pictures . . . and suddenly I had to free my hands to attend to something else. Without even thinking about it, I simply left the camera floating in mid-air, and it stayed there as if I had laid it on a table . . ."

Though it was still morning back at Cape Kennedy—which Glenn had left only less than an hour before—he had circled so much of the earth that he was already entering the dark side of it where the sun was hidden and it was night. The inhabitants down below had already had their day and were asleep. But there was no time for Glenn to sleep. He had too much to do.

It was still dark when Glenn circled around the earth and passed over Australia for the first time. Far below him, more than a hundred miles down, Glenn could see the bright lights that the Australian city of Perth had turned on to welcome him. He talked over the radio with astronaut Gordon Cooper, who had flown out to Australia by plane to communicate with Glenn from the NASA tracking station at Muchea, Australia. Cooper reminded Glenn that he would soon be picking up the lights of certain stars—Orion and Sirius, for example

—that he could use as a guide to keep track of his position.

"That was sure a short day," Glenn radioed down to Cooper as he thought about how much of the world he had just orbited in about one hour. Cooper did not quite hear the remark and asked Glenn to repeat it. "That was about the shortest day I've ever run into," Glenn said.

A few minutes after leaving Australia behind, Glenn was halfway across the wide Pacific and decided it was time to have a snack. This event was scheduled on his flight plan. Glenn was not hungry, but he was supposed to try eating in space to see

Dr. Douglas prays during one of the crises in Glenn's flight: a 4 1/2-minute communications blackout at the time of his re-entry.

if there was any difficulty in swallowing or digesting. He pulled out a tube full of applesauce, opened up the face-plate on his helmet, and squeezed the sauce into his mouth without spilling a drop.

It was almost time for Glenn's first sunrise now, and he was looking forward to it eagerly. But as he glanced out of the window and looked back toward the west, he saw the weirdest sight of his entire trip.

"At first I thought it was a sky full of stars," he said, thinking that he had somehow turned the spacecraft upside down. "But then I realized that it couldn't be because my window was pointed straight back, not up. Everywhere I looked there were thousands of tiny particles, light yellowish-green in color. It looked exactly as if the spacecraft were moving through a field of fireflies. Occasionally, one or two of them would move up slowly around the spacecraft and drift very slowly across the window before leaving. I observed the same objects for about four minutes every time the sun came up."

No one—including the Russians who had orbited the earth before Glenn—had ever reported seeing such a sight before, and Glenn was fascinated by it. He was certain that he had discovered some new phenomenon in space. At a debriefing session when he got back, he discussed what he had seen with a number of scientists and tried to figure out what the particles were. "What did they say,

John?" asked one expert jokingly.

The particles remained a deep mystery until the next Mercury mission three months later when astronaut Scott Carpenter made a similar flight and accidentally stumbled across the answer.

About 15 minutes after he saw the strange sea of green particles in the sky, John Glenn began experiencing his first trouble with the spacecraft—although there was no connection between the two occurrences. It was just that the automatic controls, which Glenn had counted on to fly the capsule while he carried out some of his experiments, were acting up.

The spacecraft would stray out of its correct position every few minutes. It would always correct itself, but each time the capsule pushed itself back into the proper position automatically it would use up precious hydrogen peroxide fuel.

This was not a serious malfunction. Glenn could turn off the faulty automatic pilot and take over the controls himself. (In fact, he had to do this in order to save the fuel for the crucial re-entry phase when he would need it most.) But the malfunction did mean that Glenn was kept so busy monitoring the controls that he had to give up some of the other experiments he had wanted to carry out. He had to cut down on picture-taking, for example; he had to cancel out another meal he had planned—a tube full of mashed roast beef; and he had to call off some scientific studies that he had wanted

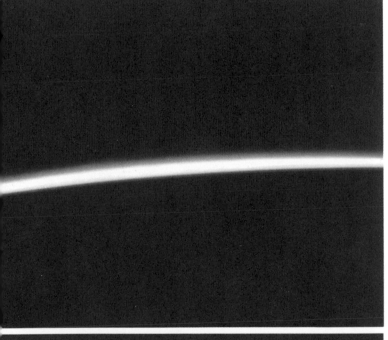

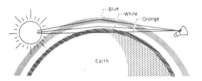

One of the purposes of the Mercury flights was to make astronomical observations. Glenn's photographs, taken at twilight, confirmed the theory that the earth's atmospheric layers reflect in different ways, resulting in bands of different colors (see diagram above). As the sun dropped below the earth's horizon (top photograph at left), Glenn's camera photographed the bands of color changing to distinct hues of blue, white, and orange (middle and bottom photographs) before being obscured by darkness. He was also told to watch for comets during this twilight period. He saw none, but he did report seeing "fireflies"—a phenomenon not fully explained until later flights.

to make of the sun and high-altitude clouds as he passed by them.

This was only one problem. There was another difficulty that John Glenn did not even know about when it first occurred. But the engineers down on the ground did; they spotted it by watching their telemetry signals—and it had them worried. According to telemetry information, the heatshield on the bottom of Glenn's capsule had somehow come loose.

The shield was programmed to do this just before the capsule hit the water in order to help cushion the shock of the landing. But it was supposed to stay tightly in place as long as Glenn was out in space in order to protect him from the intense heat that would build up around the capsule during re-entry.

This crisis was so serious that the engineers decided not to worry Glenn about it right away. There was nothing he could do about it at the moment, anyway. And the astronaut had plenty of other things on his mind that he could do something about. For one thing, the controls were beginning to act up even more.

As Glenn soared around the earth and passed into its shadow for the second time, a NASA tracking ship in the Indian Ocean asked him if he could spot any constellations of stars. Glenn had to answer that he was too busy keeping an eye on the control system just then to pay much attention to what was going on outside the window. He orbited across Australia again and out over the Pacific into his second sunrise in a little more than

When the first orbit of Friendship 7 had been completed, technicians at the Mercury Control Center received a signal indicating that something was wrong with the heatshield —a malfunction that might cause difficulty when Glenn fired the retro-rockets to slow him down and take him out of orbit (first sketch above). They ordered Glenn not to jettison the retro-rockets for fear that if they were released after firing, the entire front unit of the capsule would slip off (middle sketch). Thus, as Glenn descended, the retro-pack stayed in place, vaporizing during re-entry (last sketch). Seeing the flames pass his window, the astronaut exclaimed: ". . . that was a real fireball, boy."

John Glenn's family watches his ascent on TV. During the reentry phase, they could only trust that the heatshield would hold.

two hours. And then, after passing across the southern part of the United States, he reached the Atlantic and started on his final orbit.

As Friendship 7 crossed Africa for the third time and started out over the dark Indian Ocean, Glenn looked down and noticed a huge storm stretching out beneath him as far as he could see. Bright flashes of lightning lit up the clouds like flash bulbs going off behind wads of cotton. Then he left the storm behind him and passed over Australia for the last time.

The tension was building up now, and Gordon Cooper, in Australia, chatted with Glenn for a moment to help relieve it. Glenn radioed down that he had just completed four hours of flight time. He asked Cooper to pass the word along to his old outfit, the U.S. Marine Corps, that he expected his flight pay.

"Roger," Cooper answered. "Will do. Think they'll pay it?" "I don't know," said Glenn. "Gonna find out." "Roger. Is this flying time or rocket time?" Cooper asked. "Lighter than air," replied John Glenn with a laugh.

Glenn now reported the readings on his instrument panel to Cooper so

Soon after recovery, Glenn changed out of his space suit and had a shipboard cup of coffee.

the engineers back at Mercury control in Florida would have all the facts they needed in case of an emergency. The temperature inside the cabin was now 90 degrees. The temperature inside his suit was a comfortable 70. He had 60 per cent of his breathing oxygen left in the main tank and 90 per cent remaining in the spare tank.

Since Glenn had not even touched the reserve supply, this reading meant that 10 per cent of the oxygen in the spare tank had somehow leaked out. But he still had plenty of oxygen left, so the situation was not serious. It

was just something that the engineers needed to know about to correct the fault before the next flight.

Now it was time to start thinking about coming home. Glenn and the engineers on the ground knew from previous calculations that although he would land in the Atlantic Ocean, he would have to start slowing down while he was still out over the Pacific in order to glide down into the spot where the ships would be waiting for him. Measuring back from where the ships would be stationed, the engineers had figured that Glenn's retrorockets would have to fire exactly 2,990 miles from where he wanted to come down. It would take that long for the capsule to slow down and reenter the atmosphere at an easy angle without burning up.

And so, as Glenn zoomed past Australia for the last time, he knew there was no time to lose. He began to stow away his loose gear so it would not get in his way during the crucial descent. He also received his first real news of the heatshield problem from Gordon Cooper down below. Together Glenn and Cooper went through some testing procedures that indicated the heatshield was not really loose at all. But there was no way to make sure of this. Besides, there was nothing left to do now but come down and take the chance. If the heatshield *was* loose, John Glenn might very well burn to a crisp. But if he tried staying out in space because he was afraid the shield was loose, he would die anyway. All Glenn could do was come on in and hope for the best.

There was one final precaution which Glenn could take, however, and that was to keep the retro-rockets in place even after they had done their job of slowing him down. The three retro-rockets were joined together in a package that was attached to the center of the shield by some metal straps. The straps ran across the

Aboard the recovery ship Noa, *sailors peer over the rail at Glenn, who is dictating his flight reactions into a tape recorder. The admiring crewmen marked his first footsteps on the deck in white paint. Here, his feet are propped up on a rack of depth charges.*

shield and were fastened to the main body of the spacecraft. They were designed to break apart automatically when the retro-rockets fired and fall away along with the rockets. This would leave the heatshield flat and smooth so it could do its tricky job of soaking up the excess friction and protecting the astronaut.

But since the metal straps also held the heatshield against the main body of the spacecraft, the engineers decided to leave them in place in the hope that they would keep the shield from loosening any further. This was a quick and clever decision. And it was passed along to Glenn by radio at the right moment.

There was only one thing wrong with this sudden plan. In order to cancel out the automatic sequence that would normally break the metal straps and drop the retro-rockets, Glenn would have to shut off an automatic timer that was also designed to handle a number of other important events during re-entry. In other words, he would have to handle the re-entry maneuver on his own.

As the minutes and seconds ticked by, Glenn got set for the suspense ending. He assured the medical officers as he passed over Hawaii for the last time that he was in fine shape and ready for any emergency. Then he made contact with astronaut Wally Schirra, who was at a tracking station in California and was to give him the final countdown to fire the retro-rockets. All around the world—and

At sunset, a Navy helicopter lifts Glenn off the deck of the Noa *to the carrier* Randolph.

in front of millions of radios and TV sets in the United States—people stopped whatever they were doing to listen in utter suspense as the big moment came and the two experienced astronauts talked back and forth.

SCHIRRA: Fifteen seconds to [retro] sequence.

GLENN: Roger.

SCHIRRA: Ten [seconds to go].

SCHIRRA: Five, four, three, two, one, mark.

At this moment—a moment that was planned to last for thirty seconds —Glenn began checking to make sure that his spacecraft was in the exact position for retro-fire and that all of the important lights on his instrument panel had turned green to indicate that the equipment was ready.

GLENN: Roger. Retro sequence is green.

SCHIRRA: You have a green. You look good on attitude. (Schirra meant that he could read telemetry signals that indicated that the spacecraft was pointed at the correct angle to get the maximum braking action from the rockets.)

GLENN: Retro attitude is green.

SCHIRRA: Just past twenty. (This meant that Glenn had less than 20 seconds before the final countdown began for firing the rockets.)

GLENN: Say again.

SCHIRRA: Seconds.

GLENN: Roger.

SCHIRRA: Five, four, three, two, one, fire.

GLENN: Roger. Retros are firing. (He could feel them going off behind him.)

SCHIRRA: Sure they be.

GLENN: Are they ever. It feels like I'm going back towards Hawaii.

SCHIRRA: Don't do that. You want to go to the East Coast.

The three retro-rockets fired at the prescribed five-second intervals. And though they slowed the spacecraft down by only 500 feet per second, this was just enough to make it lose some of its momentum and start settling gradually toward the earth. As the spacecraft slowed down and started ploughing back into the thick atmosphere, the friction began building up outside the capsule and it grew hotter and hotter. John Glenn knew that if the heatshield came loose now, he would feel the intense heat first in the middle of his back. He lay helpless in his couch, waiting for the heat to build up behind him. But it never came.

Obviously, the heatshield was still intact. Glenn began to relax a little, but there was still a hair-raising ride ahead of him. He began to hear loud thumping noises behind him where the heatshield was, and he could see huge chunks of fire and red-hot material go flying past his window from the rear. Glenn assumed that this was the package of retro-rockets burning up in the white heat and falling away at last. But he could not be certain. It could be the heatshield breaking up after all, and he waited again for the intense, roasting heat to reach him.

John Glenn's heart had been beating on an average of 86 times per minute during the final hours of preparation before the flight. But now, as the re-entry phase went on and on, his pulse reached a peak of 134 beats per minute.

There was also tremendous tension in the control center. As soon as the spacecraft sliced deep into the atmosphere on its way home, a thick barrier of heat and friction built up all around it so that radio signals could not get through. The control center eventually picked up the plummeting spacecraft by radar and assumed that the capsule itself was still intact. But without being able to communicate with John Glenn himself, there was no way of knowing whether he was alive or dead.

"Hello, Cape. [This is] Friendship Seven. Over. Hello, Cape. Friendship Seven. Over." Glenn kept transmitting this message into his microphone as he plunged toward earth. But there was no answer.

Down on the ground, the men in Mercury control still could not hear Glenn's voice, and Alan Shepard stayed glued to his headset, waiting for some sign of life. "Keep talking, Al," someone said. So Shepard tried again. "Seven, this is Cape, how do you read? Over."

This time Glenn heard the transmission and radioed back immediately. "Loud and clear," he said— despite the tremendous forces buffet-

President Kennedy flew down from Washington to greet Glenn and give him the NASA Distinguished Service Medal, and to share his thumbs-up triumph (above). On February 26, he spoke to a joint session of Congress (opposite) and received a standing ovation.

ing him after hours of weightlessness. "How me?"

"Roger. Reading you loud and clear," replied a relieved Shepard. "How are you doing?" "Oh, pretty good," sighed John Glenn. "My condition is good, but that was a real fireball, boy."

Twelve seconds after that welcome conversation, John Glenn had fallen so far from orbit that he was within 80,000 feet of earth. Nineteen seconds later he had dropped to 55,000 feet. The spacecraft was rocking and swaying back and forth now as a result of

the buffeting it was taking against the thickening atmosphere. But then, the first of the capsule's two parachutes opened up to stabilize the fall.

Glenn's window was so smeared with melted resin, which had streamed back from the hot fire on his heat-shield, that he could barely see the first chute open. But it worked fine and steadied the capsule's fall until the main chute opened a little later. It slowed the spacecraft down to a

As he rode along the route of heroes, New York's Fifth Avenue, Glenn was swamped in tons of joyously thrown paper (above).

descent of only 42 feet per second. Glenn still had five minutes to go before he was due to hit the water. He contacted the recovery ships by radio and told them that he was pretty warm, but in good condition.

At last, the spacecraft bumped against the water. It sank so far under that Glenn felt he was in a submarine. Then the capsule rose to the surface again and started bobbing in the waves. Soaked with perspiration, Glenn sat waiting for the rescue.

He had landed too far from the aircraft carrier to be picked up by helicopter. But there was a destroyer stationed nearby that could haul the spacecraft out of the water by cable. This meant that to avoid flooding the spacecraft with sea water in case the destroyer's crane dropped him accidentally, Glenn had to keep the capsule's hatch closed until he was lifted to the ship's deck. He was very uncomfortable—he had forgotten to close the faceplate on his helmet during re-entry, and the temperature inside his suit was 85 degrees. The cabin temperature stood at a steaming 103 degrees.

Glenn could not see through the smeared window as the destroyer came towards him. But then, almost as if by magic, the spacecraft swung around in the water until Glenn's periscope pointed straight at the oncoming ship. He could see the sailors lined up on deck. It took a few minutes for the destroyer to come slowly alongside. But finally the spacecraft was lifted safely to the deck, and Glenn broke open the hatch and crawled out.

As soon as he could, Glenn peeled down to his underwear to cool off and asked for a glass of iced tea. The doctors on the ship weighed him immediately as part of their physical examination and discovered that he had lost almost five and a half pounds since he was launched that morning. Most of this loss, they decided, was nothing but perspiration.

The entire United States, which had sweated out John Glenn's re-entry and recovery along with him, was elated when the flight was over. And so were the engineers. Some problems had cropped up in the spacecraft that would need fixing before the next astronaut could take off. But Glenn had performed magnificently and had brought both himself and the capsule back despite all the difficulties.

He had proved that man had a definite role in space—since without the pilot, the machine might never have made it home. He had demonstrated once more that the Mercury system of space flight was basically sound and that the program could continue along the same lines the engineers had laid out.

The United States, which was thrilled by John Glenn's dramatic and heroic adventure, was at last ready to move into the space age in a big way. John Glenn's mission had helped convince the nation that Americans belonged in space.

7

THE SPACE BEYOND

Long before Glenn's spacecraft splashed into the water, flotillas of ships and fleets of airplanes and helicopters were placed in strategic spots around the world to bring the astronaut home as soon as the mission was over. The recovery ships and planes were stationed in the prime recovery area where the engineers calculated that the spacecraft would come down. And they were also waiting at scattered points in the Atlantic and Pacific where it was just possible that he might wind up if he ran into trouble and had to come down in a hurry and ahead of schedule.

This was the huge recovery operation that astronaut Alan Shepard helped to set up in the early days of the program. It was made up partly of U.S. Navy ships and helicopters that stood by in the water along the route of Glenn's orbital flight, and it also included dozens of U.S. Air Force planes that were kept on alert at airfields around the world, ready to fly to the rescue if for some reason John Glenn had to land off course. All told, several thousand sailors and aviators took part in this phase of the operation.

It was not long after John Glenn's flight that the order went out to these same sailors and aviators to stand by all over again. For though Glenn's historic and exciting flight had proved that the Mercury mission was sound, NASA's officials were still not satisfied. They had limited John Glenn to three orbits because they wanted to make sure that the Mercury space system worked before stretching it much further.

But even before Glenn was launched, the space agency was already making long-range plans for future flights into space that would take astronauts all the way to the moon and back. John Glenn had taken the first daring step along that path, but there were many more steps to take—longer steps—before the engineers could think about risking men on such missions.

For example, a flight to the moon

An Army rescue crew watches intently as Gordon Cooper, aboard Faith 7, roars into the Florida sky to begin his 34-hour ride.

126

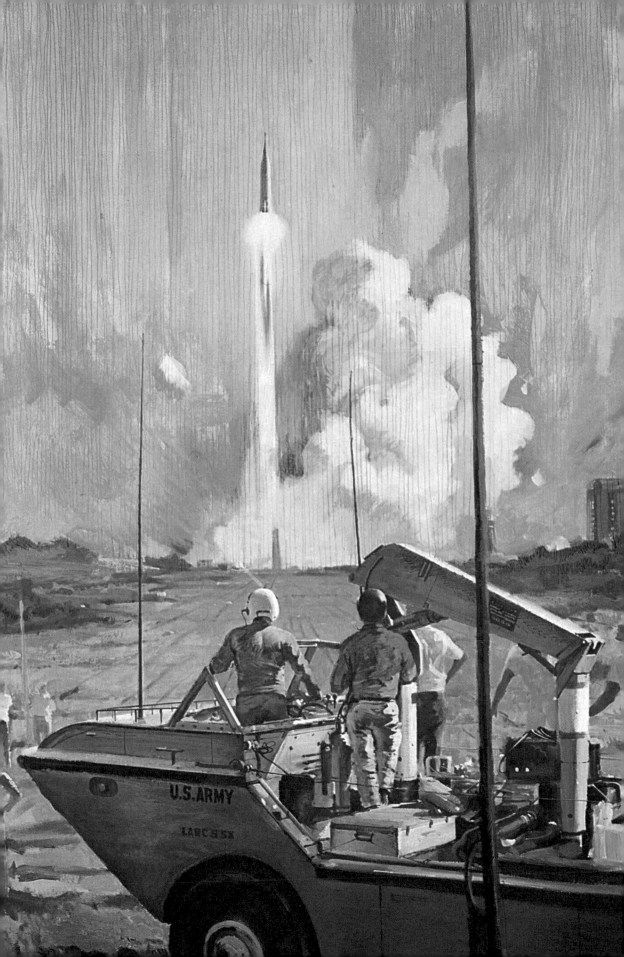

in the new spacecraft, which was to be called Apollo, would involve days of weightlessness instead of merely a few hours. The communications between the three-man Apollo spacecraft and earth would be stretched out over thousands of miles instead of just a few hundred. And there would be no tracking stations along the way to help monitor the flight or assist the pilots with their navigation. This meant that the equipment would have to work almost perfectly and that the pilots themselves would have to undergo more extensive training to prepare themselves for longer and longer flights.

As John Glenn made his ride, the equipment for the moon flights was still in the development stage and was not nearly ready for actual testing. And it would differ in many respects from the Mercury equipment which the astronauts were using to test out the basic principles of space flight.

The Apollo spacecraft that would actually take men to the moon, for example, would carry a crew of three astronauts. It would land two of them on the moon in still another craft, a smaller one, that would then return to the mother ship before the men came back to earth. In the meantime, before the Apollo launching, another spacecraft called Gemini (which means twins) would be tested. The Gemini would carry two astronauts together on training missions to prepare for the Apollo program.

All of this meant that the astronauts

MCDONNELL AIRCRAFT CORPORATION

The Gemini space capsule (above) will be the steppingstone to outer space. Manned by a crew of two, it will test the feasibility of linking units together in orbit. Opposite, engineers check the capsule's control panel.

needed more practice and that the engineers needed to learn even more about the equipment they had designed. So NASA decided to schedule three more Mercury missions to follow Glenn's. The first of these was assigned to Scott Carpenter, who had trained as Glenn's back-up pilot and was therefore ready for a mission right away. Carpenter's assignment was to repeat Glenn's three-orbit flight and see if the troublesome mechanical problems that cropped up during Glenn's mission had been solved.

After that, astronaut Walter Schirra would fly a six-orbit mission to see what happened to both the system and the astronaut when the flight time was doubled. And then, if all went well with Schirra, Gordon Cooper would stay up for 22 orbits. This was to find out if a man and the machinery could hold up under the strain of space flight for almost a day and a half.

Although it seemed to many people at the time that John Glenn had experienced the last word in adventure and daring, the flights of Carpenter, Schirra, and Cooper were also full of great moments of suspense, excitement, and human endurance. And these three flights, coupled with the missions of Shepard, Grissom, and Glenn, provided the nation with a solid foundation for future space exploration and solved many of the problems.

As it turned out, space flight was still so new when Scott Carpenter went up in Aurora 7 that he experienced several new problems. First of all, the mission was delayed for more than two weeks by several mechanical defects that showed up in the equip-

Aurora 7's flight, although less than a success, provided valuable data for the NASA scientists. They were able to study the reactions of astronaut Carpenter (above, suiting up for the launch) under the strain of attempting the first manual capsule-landing.

ment during the preflight check-out tests. But these wrinkles were eventually ironed out, and Carpenter was finally launched on the morning of May 24, 1962—about three months after Glenn's flight. The lift-off was smooth. "The first thing that impressed me when I got into orbit" Carpenter reported afterwards, "was the absolute silence of space."

But then Carpenter's troubles began. The device that was supposed to keep his spacecraft properly lined up with the horizon failed to operate correctly. And Carpenter was so anxious to accomplish his various experiments in a hurry that he used up too much of his hydrogen peroxide fuel in the first orbit. Because of this, Carpenter started to run dangerously low on fuel before the flight was over.

He realized the problem right away and tried letting his capsule drift through space without using the controls at all. There was no danger in this: the capsule was on a predetermined path and could not leave it until the retro-rockets slowed it down. But, even so, Carpenter had to cut down on some of his experiments in order to save fuel.

This was not the only problem. Carpenter's space suit became overheated during the early part of his flight, making him extremely uncomfortable. As a result of this crisis, he brought back some ideas on how the suit could be improved for future flights so other astronauts would not suffer from the same difficulty. This, of course, had been a major reason for the flight.

Scott Carpenter also solved the mystery of John Glenn's fireflies. This discovery came near the end of his flight and it happened entirely by accident. Carpenter was passing over Hawaii on his third and final orbit and was trying to do several things at once. He had to maneuver the capsule into position to get some pictures of the sunrise. He was trying to stow his equipment away so it would not bounce around during re-entry. And he was also communicating with the Hawaii tracking station about the exact timing of his retro-rockets. Suddenly, in the midst of all this work, one of the small luminous particles went floating past his window. Carpenter had seen the particles before on previous orbits, but he had not been able to get a picture of them.

"I reached out to grab the light meter to make a reading," he said. "As I did this, I hit my hand against the wall of the cabin. A whole cloud of particles flew off past the window. This was such a surprise that I started banging the wall all around me. Every time I hit it, more particles flew off. I was pretty sure from this that they were coming from the capsule itself, and not from other sources as John had thought." The engineers agreed with Carpenter's findings and decided that the particles were small bits of frost that collected on the spacecraft and then fell off again as it drifted along through space. They were trailing along in the capsule's orbital path

in much the same way as Jules Verne's dead dog.

The greatest fear that had plagued John Glenn—the loose heatshield—did not reoccur during Carpenter's flight. But he had a hard time getting back to earth, too. He landed so far from the rescue ships that for a long time many people feared he was lost. His troubles began when the retro-rockets failed to go off on schedule, as they were supposed to do automatically. As soon as he realized this, Carpenter had to push a button to fire the rockets. But this caused about a three-second delay in the firing.

Since the capsule was going at a

On board the Intrepid, *one of the doctors (at right above) carries out additional tests on Scott Carpenter after his delayed rescue.*

131

speed of 5 miles per second, this error meant he would land 15 miles beyond the recovery area where the ships were. But this was only part of the problem. When they did go off, the retro-rockets did not produce as much braking action as they were supposed to. This meant that the spacecraft did not slow down enough and went coasting another 60 miles beyond the recovery area—for a total error now of 75 miles. Then, on top of all this, the spacecraft had not been positioned in exactly the precise attitude for re-entry when the rockets went off. Instead of being lined up perfectly along the direction of flight, it was slanted slightly off course. Thus, the retro-rockets fired at the wrong angle, adding so much extra mileage to the flight that Carpenter overshot the recovery fleet by a total of 250 miles.

Because of this error, Carpenter and Aurora 7 landed in the water completely out of range of both the shipboard helicopters and the standby craft that were waiting for them. The engineers in the control center had been able to compute the general area Carpenter would land in by watching his descent on radar. They immediately dispatched some land-based Navy planes to search for him in the water. They also sent a radio message to Carpenter, telling him to be patient because it might take quite a while for rescuers to reach him.

The landing itself was not too rough. Carpenter's capsule dunked itself under water and then keeled over

Sigma 7 landed with the help of a single parachute

The big Apollo spacecraft will need two parachutes.

on its side just as all the others had. Then it righted itself and started to bob about on top of the small waves. Carpenter could see some drops of water inside his spacecraft. This meant the capsule might be leaking, so he decided it would be a good idea to climb out and get into the emergency raft that he could toss out ahead of him.

He did not have to open up the side hatch that might let in more water. Carpenter has thin hips, and he was able to crawl up through a narrow passage in the top of the spacecraft, push the life raft out ahead of him, and climb into it as soon as it inflated in the water. Taking with him only the camera he had used to record some of the strange sights of space, Carpenter waited patiently until Navy frogmen were parachuted into the water from low-flying airplanes. Carpenter talked with the frogmen as they splashed around attaching special gear to the spacecraft to keep it afloat. And three hours after he had hit the water, Carpenter himself was picked up by a seaplane that landed nearby.

The spacecraft was picked up later. It had not been a perfect flight, but Carpenter had managed to overcome his problems and save both himself and the spacecraft full of instruments. And NASA experts decided, after studying the record of the flight, that they could safely move on to the next step.

The next step toward the forthcoming Apollo and Gemini flights was taken on October 3, 1962. As a test of U.S. technological skills it was almost perfect in every way. The pilot was astronaut Wally Schirra, and the plan called for his Sigma 7 to orbit the earth six times to double the distance that Glenn and Carpenter had flown and see what happened.

The lift-off was smooth. The Atlas that put Schirra into orbit produced just a shade more speed than it was supposed to—about 15 feet per second extra—and as a result of this extra thrust Schirra reached a peak altitude of 152.8 miles, about 8-1/2 miles higher than the engineers had planned for him to go. This presented no problem, however. Back at the Goddard Space Flight Center in Maryland, which was named for the American rocket pioneer, big electronic computers kept track of the flight and quickly figured out how to correct for this extra speed so that Schirra could still time his return and come down at the right place in the Pacific where the ships would be waiting.

Just as Glenn and Carpenter had done, Schirra spent the first part of his flight getting himself adjusted to the strange feeling of weightlessness and testing the controls.

The only problem that Schirra ran into on his entire flight cropped up as he was passing over Africa on his first orbit. His suit began to heat up, much as Scott Carpenter's suit had done. And it took Schirra about two hours of patient fiddling with the control knobs before he felt comfortable. At one point, the engineers on the ground were considering the idea of bringing Schirra home before his mission was completed. This was because they received some faulty telemetry readings that indicated Schirra was a lot warmer inside his suit than he actually was. After talking it over with Schirra by radio, however, the engineers agreed to let him keep going.

The engineers were happy to continue the mission because they had counted on it to test out several ideas that they had not been able to try on previous flights. They had adjusted the controls, for example, so that some of the little hydrogen peroxide jets could not switch on automatically and waste precious fuel as they had done on previous flights. They had attached

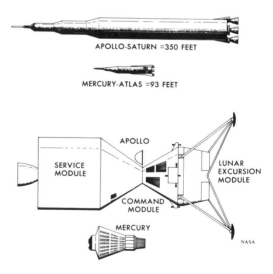

The one-man Mercury capsule and its Atlas rocket will be dwarfed by the spaceships of tomorrow. The Apollo lunar excursion module (LEM) will carry three men and will ride into orbit on the mighty Saturn V rocket.

small samples of various metals to the outer skin of the capsule to see how well each sample stood up against the tremendous heat of re-entry. They hoped to get ideas from this on how to build the Apollo spacecraft and other spaceships of the future. They provided Schirra with a new kind of microphone inside his helmet that they believed would provide better communications than they had had on previous missions. And they had also rigged a new kind of antenna on the outside of the capsule to increase the range of the capsule's radio. In addition to these experiments, Schirra carried a special camera and several different kinds of film in order to make pictures of high-altitude clouds for the weather experts.

One of the main purposes of Schirra's flight, however, was simply to see how skillfully he could fly the mission without using too much electrical power and too much of Sigma 7's control fuels. If he could cut the use of these supplies to a minimum, then the engineers knew they could use the same spacecraft for even longer flights without having to add heavy reinforcements.

Schirra performed this task beautifully. At the end of his first orbit, even with all the maneuvers he had to carry out to test the controls, he still had 98 per cent of his fuel left for the remaining five orbits. Schirra accomplished this feat partly by shutting down the controls altogether during long portions of the flight and allowing the spacecraft to drift. This system worked fine, and it proved that other astronauts could go up later for even longer missions with no increase in the load of fuel.

Several hours later, at the end of his fourth orbit, Schirra still had 86 per cent of his fuel left in the main tank and 98 per cent left in the reserve supply. The engineers down on the ground were very pleased.

As Schirra neared the end of his mission and was getting set for his last sunrise of the day, he lined his spacecraft up in the correct position for re-entry by aiming it at several stars and planets, including Jupiter. Then exactly 8 hours, 51 minutes, and 28 seconds after Schirra had left the ground, the retro-rocket procedure began automatically and right on schedule. Unlike Glenn and Carpenter, Schirra did not have to take over the controls. His spacecraft was working beautifully and handled the job itself.

There was no problem at all during the descent. All of the events ticked off right on schedule without any emergencies. After his first small parachute and second main chute broke out on schedule, Schirra swung seaward to make an almost perfect, bullseye landing. He was only about four miles from where the big aircraft carrier *Kearsarge* was waiting for him.

As the Navy frogmen jumped into the water to buoy up the spacecraft with inflatable rafts, Schirra stayed inside to avoid opening the hatch. The

Cascading water, Sigma 7 is hoisted aboard the U.S.S. Kearsarge *only 39 minutes after landing. Though some equipment small and large—like the* Kearsarge*—was left over from World War II, the scientists developed many all-new systems for Project Mercury and for the space programs of the future.*

carrier moved in closer and finally nudged alongside the bobbing spacecraft and lifted it by cable to the deck. Schirra, who had served on carriers before as a Naval aviator, was happy to be back aboard a big Navy ship.

The high point of Gordon Cooper's life came on the morning of May 15, 1963, when he crawled into Faith 7 for the longest ride of all the astronaut missions—22 orbits—a journey

that would keep him weightless in space for nearly 34 hours.

For many months before this morning finally came, Cooper trained hard for the flight, and the engineers fussed over the spacecraft and the big Atlas that would lift it into orbit. The flight was postponed for several weeks at one point when the engineers discovered some wiring problems inside the Atlas rocket when they tested it at the Convair factory in San Diego, California. During this delay, Cooper went on practicing, spending hours in the training devices that helped him rehearse each minute of a mission from start to finish.

Then, in May, the flight had to be delayed once more for what seemed like a stupid reason at the time. Everything was perfect with the capsule and the Atlas, but the old-fashioned diesel engine that was supposed to pull the gantry back from the Atlas refused to work! Cooper had been locked up for hours inside the spacecraft when the delay came, but he took it with a smile and climbed back in the next day to try again.

This time everything went fine. The flight Cooper flew was almost perfect. The engineers had placed some extra padding around his helmet to cut down on the vibrations during lift-off. And despite the tremendous power of the Atlas, Cooper said it was just like riding in a fast car or speedboat with the full throttle on. He admitted that he felt a little strange when the spacecraft finally went into orbit and

INJECTION

PARKING ORBIT

LUNAR TRAJECTORY

A vital stage in future space flights will be the "parking orbit," which will allow the Apollo-Saturn vehicle (above) to wait for the right moment to begin its lunar journey.

he was suddenly weightless. But he soon grew used to this sensation—so used to it, in fact, that later on he had no trouble at all relaxing and falling asleep. During the first few minutes, however, he could not help concentrating on the fantastic sights he saw through the window.

Then Cooper settled down to his work. He described the vivid colors in the narrow band of light that rims the earth during sunrise and sunset. And as soon as it got dark he started ticking off the stars that he recognized in the night sky south of India. "There's Orion," he said, "and Betelgeuse. What a beautiful night tonight." Before the flight was over, he would have almost 24 more nights.

Cooper was as careful as Schirra had been not to use too much of his fuel as he handled the controls. He also used up so little oxygen in the breathing tanks that the engineers down below jokingly told him he could stop holding his breath. Actually, Cooper was breathing normally, but the equipment was working so efficiently that he did not have to draw so heavily on the supplies of oxygen as some of the other astronauts had.

Yet the flight was not routine by any means. Cooper had to keep on his toes for emergencies, and naturally there was strain involved in spending so long in a strange environment. But Cooper obviously enjoyed every minute of it. He had better visibility than the other astronauts who had orbited ahead of him. And he spent much time pinpointing objects on earth. "I could spot houses in Asia by following the smoke down to the chimneys," he said. "I could see the dust blowing off a road, and then find the road. I found a steam locomotive puffing along in northern India by seeing the smoke and then the railroad tracks and finally the engine."

But Cooper had much more to do than merely gaze at the scenery. He knew that an emergency could crop up that might force him to start re-entry procedures and head back to earth on a moment's notice.

In addition to the main recovery fleet in the Pacific, where Cooper planned to land if everything went well, the U.S. Navy and Air Force

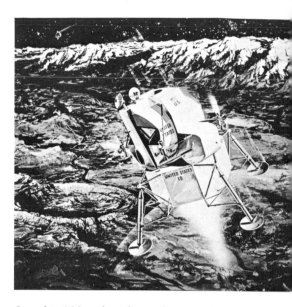

In orbit 100 miles above the moon's equator, the crew of the Apollo will crawl from the mother ship into the landing craft (cutaway view opposite) that will take them down to the moon. The engine of the leggy vehicle will then be fired to brake the touchdown (above). With their mission completed, the astronauts will blast-off for a rendezvous with the mother ship, using the base of the landing craft as a launching pad (below).

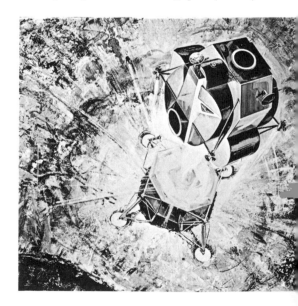

had scattered emergency facilities all around the world to help rescue Cooper in case he had to come down ahead of time. As he approached each of these areas, Cooper had to run through a set routine of procedures just to be ready for a quick re-entry in case of trouble.

He also had a number of experiments to carry out. One of these involved tossing out into space a beacon with a flashing light attached to it. Since the beacon was now weightless, it trailed along behind the capsule in the same orbital path. Cooper's job was to keep his eye on the beacon from time to time to test his ability to judge distances between objects in space.

The purpose of this experiment was to prepare for future missions to the moon and back when the astronauts would have to find and link up with other spacecraft. Cooper was also supposed to eject a balloon from the capsule and drag it along behind. This was partly to give him more practice in judging distances and also to see how dense the air was in space and how it affected the balloon's flight.

Unfortunately, the balloon experiment failed to work. And at one point during the flight when engineers on the ground asked how he was doing with the beacon, Cooper laughed and reported, "I was up with the little rascal all last night." Cooper judged that the distance between the spacecraft and its satellite beacon varied between 7 and 16 miles or so, and that it was about as bright as a dim star. He knew it was the beacon and not a star from the way it flashed off and on. Out where Cooper was, beyond the earth's atmosphere, the stars did not twinkle. But looking down on earth through the heavy atmosphere, Cooper noticed that now it was the lights on earth that twinkled. The atmosphere was now blocking out Cooper's view of the earth.

Cooper spent a good deal of time taking pictures of the earth and the clouds with the special cameras he took along. He carefully read off a description of each picture into a tape recorder so the experts could determine later exactly where and when it was taken. He also tried out a new kind of dehydrated food that NASA experts hoped would help feed astronauts on future flights. (Cooper had a little trouble with this experiment. He had to pour water into the plastic bags holding the powdered food in order to make it edible. But the water kept spilling, and huge drops of it got away from Cooper and went drifting around in the cockpit where he could not mop them up.)

He also held his breath from time to time so the doctors down below could measure his blood pressure over the telemetry circuit. A special instrument strapped to his arm gave them the reading. "Here's a full breath," he announced over the radio as he passed over the tracking station in Zanzibar. "Very good," the doctor radioed back. "That's just what our recordings show here." In other words, the doctors could tell even hundreds of miles away whether Cooper was breathing or not.

Cooper was very good-natured about all of the chores he had to do. He knew that the engineers wanted to gather a maximum amount of information from his flight, and he was more than willing to cooperate.

Only once did the spacecraft pull a major surprise on the astronaut. It happened on the nineteenth orbit, when the flight had only about four hours left to go. A light suddenly flashed on the instrument panel. It indicated that the spacecraft had automatically begun a series of maneuvers that were not supposed to occur until after the retro-rockets had fired and the spacecraft was already well on its way home.

This was serious. For if these events were taking place now, it would only mean a complete waste of the fuel that was being used to carry them out. Cooper quickly switched off some of the automatic controls to prevent this from happening. This meant, of course, that with some of the controls

turned off, Cooper would have to perform these functions himself later on.

The engineers down below were
disappointed at this turn of events,
for they had hoped that they had
eliminated all such mechanical bugs.
But the problem did not really bother
Cooper at all. As far as he was concerned, this was precisely what he was
up here for—to take over as a trained
pilot and fly the capsule when the
machines failed.

During the final two orbits, Cooper
began stashing away the loose gear
and taking bearings on the stars so
his spacecraft would be perfectly
lined up for the retro-rockets to fire.
He had to do this manually, but he
was all set in plenty of time. Then the
spacecraft pulled another unexpected
trick on him. Cooper had counted on
switching over to the automatic pilot
long enough to hold the spacecraft in
its proper position during the actual
re-entry. He felt that this would be
more accurate. But when he tried to
start up the autopilot he discovered
there was no power to run it. He tried
the reserve source of power, but this

*After the triumphant completion of Gordon
Cooper's 22-orbit ride in space, NASA art-
ist Mitchell Jamieson made several sketches
of the astronaut on an orbital map (left).*

OVERLEAF: *Whipping the waves into foam
with the downdraft of its rotors, one of the
helicopters from the* Kearsarge *hovers over
Cooper's capsule during recovery operations.*

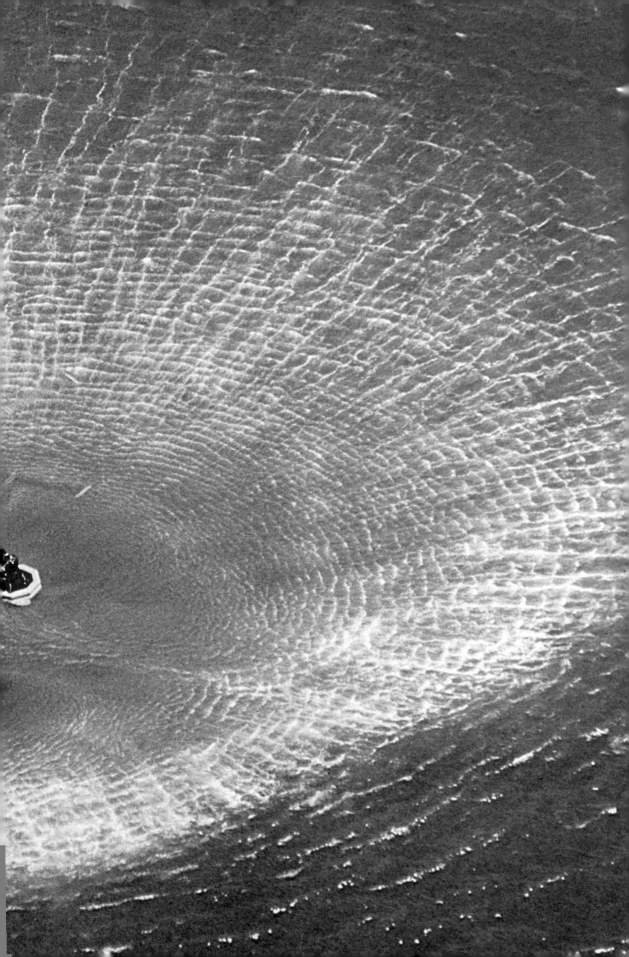

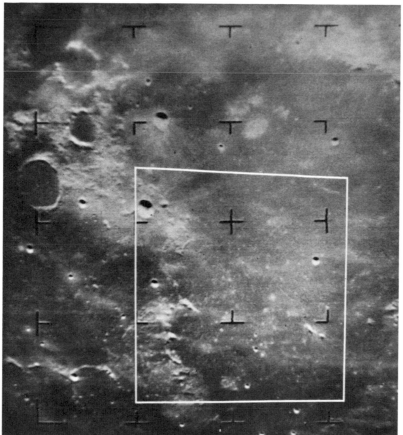

failed him too. (The engineers found out later during their postflight inspection of the capsule that moisture had collected in both power sources and shorted them out.) Now Cooper knew he would have to perform all of the re-entry maneuvers by himself.

Gordon Cooper had enough confidence in his abilities as a pilot to know he could handle this emergency. In fact, he had spent a lot of time before the mission flying fast, complicated military jets just to keep in practice for the kind of split-second timing he would need in the spacecraft. He had also dozed off for several naps during the mission, and he felt completely rested for whatever problems he had to face now.

He slept for a total of more than four hours during the flight, and he said later that he believed he slept more soundly in space than on the ground. The only thing that worried him about his naps was that his weightless arms kept stretching out in

America's space research has shed light in many areas. Ranger VII sent close-ups of the moon, like the view of Mare Nubian (above at left), while Cooper's photograph of the Himalayas (above) provided geologists with information that was never available before.

the list of re-entry procedures with Cooper and read him the correct elapsed time of the mission so he could check it against the electric timer on his instrument panel. From the moment of lift-off at Cape Kennedy, Cooper had been up for a total of 33 hours, 57 minutes, and 6 seconds. There were still about 23 minutes to go before he splashed down in the ocean. Cooper assured Shepard that he had the spacecraft lined up in the proper attitude for the retro-rockets to fire and slow him down.

"I'm looking for a lot of experience on this flight," Cooper added— referring to the fact that he would have to control the spacecraft manually the rest of the way home. "You're going to get it," said Shepard reassuringly.

Then Scott Carpenter took over from the tracking station farther east at Hawaii and informed Cooper what the weather would be like in the landing area. There would be some clouds at 1,500 feet, Carpenter said, plus a mild surface wind and waves about five feet high.

Finally, the exact moment came for the retro-rockets to fire. They went off on schedule, and Cooper held the spacecraft steady as it started to slow down and cut into the atmosphere. The parachutes broke open right on time to help stabilize the descent. And Cooper described each event with cool precision so that the engineers and the other astronauts who were following his progress as he descend-

front of him when he went to sleep. He finally tucked his hands under the straps of his harness so they would not accidentally bump into the instrument panel and push some button that was not supposed to be pushed.

Al Shepard, who was stationed on a tracking ship in the Pacific, went over

ed would know what was going on.

From his desk at the Hawaii tracking station, Scott Carpenter kept up a flow of conversation with Cooper and went down the checklist of things to do. He reminded Cooper to unfasten his helmet at the prescribed moment and to tighten his landing straps just before impact in the water. Cooper, meanwhile, was performing his pilot functions so perfectly that sailors on the big carrier *Kearsarge* —the same ship that had picked up Schirra—could see the capsule coming down by its main parachute only a few miles away.

"We are circling you at five hundred feet," said the pilot of a helicopter that followed Cooper as he drifted down. "You're coming down very nicely. The sea state is about five to eight foot waves, a few white caps. The wind is just perfect. The carrier is about three miles away. Couldn't be a nicer shot."

As soon as Cooper's capsule hit the water, frogmen jumped in after it to keep it afloat with their inflatable rafts. "Hello dahr, how are you?" Cooper shouted to the swimmers. "I would like to come aboard the carrier if they will grant permission for an Air Force officer," Cooper joked. Permission was quickly granted. And

within 40 minutes Cooper's spacecraft was being lifted to the deck of the ship with Cooper still inside it.

Cooper was a little wobbly as he crawled through the hatch and stepped out onto the ship. His ears were cracking from the long flight. He was tired and felt a little dizzy from being cooped up for so long. He was also extremely thirsty from sweating off nearly eight pounds of perspiration,

Pad 14 at Cape Kennedy, the starting point for Gordon Cooper's dramatic ride into history, stands lifeless and alone—its role in the race for space now a part of yesterday.

146

some of which now soaked his underwear and the suit. But after a sleep of about nine hours on board the carrier, Cooper was back to his old self again and ready to start briefing the NASA experts who were on the carrier about the details of his flight.

Cooper had enough details to keep the engineers busy digesting them for weeks. He had completed the longest flight any American had ever made. He had proved once more that trained pilots are necessary in space to make the complex spacecraft perform at its best. And he had helped solve so many of the problems and worries the engineers had about their flight system that NASA decided—on the basis of Cooper's great success—to call off any further Mercury missions and get on with bigger plans for flights to the moon and beyond.

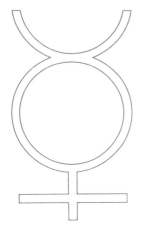

Mercury, the planet nearest the sun, gave its name and symbol (above) to the project that put the first Americans into orbit.

AMERICAN HERITAGE PUBLISHING CO., INC.

PRESIDENT JAMES PARTON
EDITOR IN CHIEF JOSEPH J. THORNDIKE, JR.
EDITORIAL DIRECTOR, BOOK DIVISION RICHARD M. KETCHUM
ART DIRECTOR IRWIN GLUSKER

AMERICAN HERITAGE JUNIOR LIBRARY

EDITOR RUSSELL BOURNE
ASSISTANT EDITOR SEAN MORRISON
ART DIRECTOR JANET CZARNETZKI
PICTURE RESEARCHER MARY LEVERTY
COPY EDITOR ELAINE ANDREWS
COPY EDITOR BARBARA FISHER SHOR
EDITORIAL ASSISTANT NANCY SIMON
EDITORIAL ASSISTANT BETSY SANDERS

ACKNOWLEDGMENTS

The Editors are deeply grateful to Frederick C. Durant III, Assistant Director for Astronautics, National Air Museum, for his guidance and advice on the manuscript as well as on pictorial material and sources. They would also like to express their appreciation to Mrs. Robert Goddard for her kind cooperation. In addition, the Editors wish to thank the following individuals and organizations for their assistance in preparing this book:

Department of the Air Force—Lieutenant Colonel C. V. Glines, Major L. Peterson, Mrs. Frances Lewis
Department of the Navy—Lieutenant Commander D. K. Dagle, Charles Lawrence
National Aeronautics and Space Administration—Les Gaver, Shelby Thompson, James Dean
National Air Museum, Smithsonian Institution—S. Paul Johnston, Robert B. Wood
Susanne Puddefoot, London
Victor Louis, Moscow
Diagrams by Herbert S. Borst. Map by Argenziano Assoc.

148

FURTHER READING

Alexander, Thomas. *Project Apollo; Man to the Moon.* New York, Harper & Brothers, 1964.

Bergaust, Erik. *Reaching for the Stars.* New York, Doubleday, 1960.

Butterworth, W. E. *The Wonders of Rockets and Missiles.* New York, G. P. Putnam's Sons, 1964.

Canby, Courtland. *A History of Rockets and Space.* New York, Hawthorn, 1963.

Clarke, Arthur C. *The Exploration of Space.* New York, Harper & Brothers, 1960.

King, Henry C. *Our World in Space.* Philadelphia, Macrae, 1964.

Lehman, Milton. *This High Man.* New York, Farrar, Straus, 1963.

Ley, Willy. *Our Work in Space.* New York, Macmillan, 1963.

———*Rockets, Missiles and Space Travel.* New York, Viking, 1961.

Man and Space. (ed. *Life* Magazine). Time, Inc. 1964.

Ronan, Colin A. *Man Probes the Universe.* Garden City, N.Y., Natural History Press, 1964.

Stoiko, Michael. *Project Gemini.* New York, Holt, Rinehart & Winston, 1963.

Thomas, Shirley. *Men of Space.* Philadelphia, Chilton, 1961.

Verne, Jules. *From the Earth to the Moon.* New York, Scribner's Sons, 1912.

Von Braun, Wernher. *First Men to the Moon.* New York, Holt, Rinehart & Winston, 1960.

Wells, H. G. *The War of the Worlds.* New York, Random House, 1960.

Williams, Beryl, and Epstein, Samuel. *The Rocket Pioneers.* New York, Julian Messner, 1955.

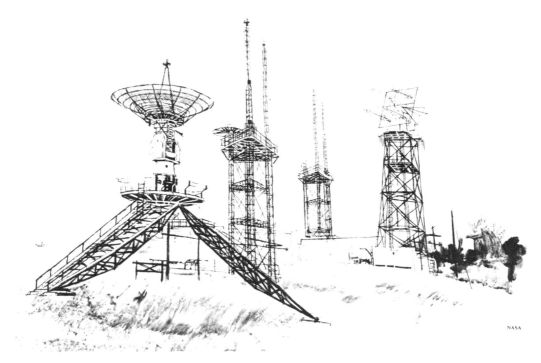

Standing like attentive insects outside of the Command Destruct Building at Cape Kennedy, these devices send the "destruct" command to rockets should there be any malfunction.

INDEX

Bold face indicates pages on which illustrations appear